——Basic Chinese

主编 刘元满
作者 王添淼

人民教育出版社
·北京·

图书在版编目(CIP)数据

中文在手:汉英对照版.基础篇/刘元满主编.—北京:人民教育出版社,2013.6
ISBN 978-7-107-25903-6

Ⅰ.①中… Ⅱ.①刘… Ⅲ.①汉语—对外汉语教学—自学参考资料 Ⅳ.①H195.4

中国版本图书馆CIP数据核字(2013)第136858号

人民教育出版社 出版发行
网址:http://www.pep.com.cn
北京恒艺博缘印务有限公司印装 全国新华书店经销
2013年8月第1版 2013年8月第1次印刷
开本:890毫米×1 240毫米 1/48 印张:4.25
字数:85千字 印数:0 001~3 000册
审图号:GS(2013)1834号
定价:40.00元(附MP3光盘1张)
著作权所有·请勿擅用本书制作各类出版物·违者必究
如发现印、装质量问题,影响阅读,请与本社出版科联系调换。
(联系地址:北京市海淀区中关村南大街17号院1号楼 邮编:100081)

前 言

* * *

《汉语2008》多语种系列丛书自2007年出版以来，满足了相应的市场需求，得到了使用者的充分肯定。许多使用者借此增强了汉语交际能力，更多地了解了现实中的中国。时间在推移，社会在前进，丛书中的一些内容也需要与时俱进，及时更新。于是，我们对这套丛书进行了修订，并更名为《中文在手》（*CHINESE IN HAND*），其目的正如书名所示，希望读者既能拿在手里随时应急或学习，便捷地解决实际生活中的一些交际问题，又能通过该书学会更地道的汉语表达，进而掌握中文。此次修订，包括"基础篇""生活篇""旅游篇""交通篇"4种，课文全部经过调整，部分课文完全重写，一些小知识也相应更新，同时采纳读者建议，增设生词表，方便读者查阅。

《中文在手》系列丛书主要面向来华旅游、学习、工作的外国人和希望学习汉语、了解中国的外国朋友。整套丛书注重实用性、趣味性，兼顾科学性，突出时代感。所展示的日常交际用语和实用情景对话，基本可以满足外国人在中国的日常交际需要。该丛书既可以作为汉语实用交际手册，又可以作为专题式短期汉语教材使用。

丛书以"整句输入"为特色，每册书围绕几名来中国短期工作、生活的外国人，展现他们在常见场景中的交际活动。丛书每册20课,每课由5部分组成:(1)6个基本句。从每课的会话中提取而来,即学即用。(2)2~3段会话。会话以场景为依托,按照人物的身份、关系编写,使用简洁、得体的口语表达,同时有意在场景中安排一些常见的功能项目,突出交际性。(3)生词表。从会话中选取一些字面上不易直接了解的词语进行标注。(4)扩展词语。补充一些与该课内容相关的常用词语,丰富、拓展读者的表达。(5)小知识。选取与该课内容有关的当代中国地理、历史、文化和生活常识等背景知识,从而使读者能更顺畅地与中国人交往,更好地融入到中国人的生活中。

《中文在手》中的基本句、会话和扩展词语均采用拼音、汉字和外语相对照的形式,方便读者理解学习。小知识全部用外语呈现。丛书采用48开的纸型设计,读者一册在握,便于携带。每册书均配有光盘。为方便读者更好地学习和使用,本丛书同时推出数字版本,可下载到移动终端使用。

本套丛书由人民教育出版社课程教材研究所汉语课程教材研究开发中心策划组织,北京大学刘元满教授担任主编,各册编者充分发挥他们丰富的教学智慧,使其质量有了极大保证。我们真诚地希望本套丛书成为外国朋友在中国生活、旅行和学习的必备用书。

《中文在手·基础篇》(汉英对照版)作者王添淼。翻译蒋虹、李瑜。责任编辑张君。审稿狄国伟、董蔚君。英文审稿Miriam Ruth Fisher。封面及版式设计蒋宏工作室。插图制作高岱。

人民教育出版社　课程教材研究所
汉语课程教材研究开发中心
2013年6月

Preface

The multi-lingual series *Chinese 2008* has been satisfying market demand since its publication in 2007, with full endorsement from its users. Many users have enhanced their Chinese communicative competence and thereby acquired a better understanding of the realities of China. As time and society have progressed, however, the renewal of some parts of this series has become necessary. As a result we have revised this series and changed its name to *Chinese in Hand*. As is shown in the name of the book, our primary goal is to enable the readers to use it whenever necessary to solve communication problems in real life and to master the Chinese language by learning authentic expressions. This revised version includes four separate books: *Basic Chinese, Daily Chinese, Travel Chinese* and *Transportation Chinese*. All the texts have been revised, and some texts have been fully rewritten. Some of the tips have also been replaced accordingly. New word lists have been added to the chapters at the suggestion of readers.

The target readers are those foreigners who come to China to travel, study or work, and those who hope to learn Chinese and explore China. Much attention has been paid to ensuring that this series be not only practical and interesting, but also encourage the latest scientific knowledge and be up-to-date. The daily communication expressions and practical situational conversations in this series cover the basic needs of non-Chinese visitors in their daily communication in China. This series, as a practical Chinese communication handbook, can also serve as a textbook for short-term training programs.

Whole-sentence-input is the special feature of this series. Each book is based on the common situational activities of a few foreigners who come to work in China short term. Each book has twenty lessons, and each lesson consists of five sections. The first section contains six basic sentences, which are taken from the dialogues in each lesson and can be used directly in real life. The second section consists of two or three dialogues developed from related situations. In these dialogues, simple and appropriate expressions are used according to the status of the speakers and the relations between them. Meanwhile, some popular functional items are set in these situations to emphasize their communicative nature. The third section is "New Words". Some hard words for foreigners are chosen from each lesson to be explained and phonetically marked. The fourth section is "Additional Expressions". It includes frequently used words and expressions related to the situations presented in the lessons and serves to enhance the readers' ability to express themselves. The last section, called "Tip", provides some general information about geography, history, culture and general knowledge of everyday life in contemporary China in an attempt to enable the readers to better associate and mix with the Chinese people.

For readers' convenience, *pinyin*, Chinese

characters and English equivalents are provided in the Basic Sentences, Dialogues, New Words and Additional Expressions in each book of *Chinese in Hand*. All the "Tip" are in English to allow readers to understand the information easily. Printed as small paperbacks, all the books are easy for readers to carry around. All books are supplied with CDs. The digital version of this series will be introduced in the App Store at the time of publishing to better facilitate the readers' use and study.

The Chinese as a Foreign Language Education Editorial Department of the People's Education Press is the designer and organizer of this series, with Professor Liu Yuanman as the chief editor. The editors, with a wealth of teaching wisdom, have worked hard to ensure the quality of this series. We sincerely hope that this series will continue to be indispensible to our foreign friends who live, travel and study in China.

Chinese in Hand: *Basic Chinese* (Chinese-English Version)

Writer: Wang Tianmiao

Translator: Jiang Hong, Li Yu

Executive Editor: Zhang Jun

Reviewer: Di Guowei, Dong Weijun

English Reviewer: Miriam Ruth Fisher

Cover and Format Design: Jiang Hong Workshop

Illustration by Gao Dai.

Chinese as a Foreign Language Education Editorial Department
Curriculum & Teaching Materials Research Institute
People's Education Press
June, 2013

zhǔyào rénwù jièshào
主要人物介绍
Introduction to the Main Characters

Mǎkè
马克

Mark, a Frenchman, works in a Chinese company.

Wáng Míng
王明

A Chinese man, a good friend of Mark's, does art research.

Bái Méi
白梅

May, an American woman, teaches English in Beijing, often helps interpret for Wang Ming.

Wáng Ān'ān
王安安

A Chinese woman, a friend of Mark's when he was a foreign student.

mùlù
目 录
CONTENTS

1 wènhòu hé dǎ zhāohu
问候和打招呼 1
Greetings
Tip: Chinese Ways of Greeting

2 jièshào
介绍 9
Introduction
Tip: Chinese Names

3 xúnwèn
询问 17
Inquiry
Tip: Currency

4 yāoqǐng hé yuēdìng
邀请和约定 25
Invitations and Appointments
Tip: Beijing Opera

5 求助 qiúzhù ... 33
Asking for Help
Tip: Telephone Numbers for Assistance in China

6 看病 kànbìng ... 41
Seeing a Doctor
Tip: Flow Chart in a Hospital

7 感谢和道歉 gǎnxiè hé dàoqiàn ... 49
Thanks and Apology
Tip: Giving Presents in China

8 称赞 chēngzàn ... 57
Compliments
Tip: Chinese Response to Praise

9 祝贺 zhùhè ... 67
Congratulations
Tip: Occasions on Which Chinese Invite People to Dinner

10 chéng fēijī
乘飞机 ·················· 73
Taking a Plane
Tip: Major Airlines

11 chéng huǒchē
乘火车 ·················· 81
Taking a Train
Tip: Train Types and Speed in China

12 chéngzuò shì nèi jiāotōng gōngjù
乘坐市内交通工具 ··· 89
Taking Public Transportation in the City
Tip: Subways in China

13 zài jiǔdiàn
在酒店 ·················· 99
At the Hotel
Tip: Some Five-star Hotels in Beijing

14 cānyǐn
餐饮 ···················· 111
Restaurants
Tip: Some Famous Restaurants in Beijing

15 打电话 dǎ diànhuà 119
Making Telephone Calls

Tip: Making International Calls with Mobile Phones in China

16 购物 gòuwù 129
Shopping

Tip: Classification of Shopping Centers in China

17 逛街 guàng jiē 141
Strolling Around

Tip: Chinese Traditional Food

18 做客 zuòkè 151
Being a Guest

Tip: Being a Good Guest in China

19 谈天气 tán tiānqì 163
Talking About Weather

Tip: China's Climate

20 sòngxíng 送行 171
Seeing Off

Tip: Four Treasures of the Study

fùlù 附录 183
Appendices

I 中国著名连锁酒店 Zhōngguó zhùmíng liánsuǒ jiǔdiàn 183
Well-known Hotel Chains in China

II 北京各类市场 Běijīng gè lèi shìchǎng 185
Various Markets in Beijing

III 中国行政区划 Zhōngguó xíngzhèng qūhuà
Administrative Divisions of China

wènhòu hé dǎ zhāohu
问候和打招呼
Greetings

Basic Sentences

Rènshi nǐ hěn gāoxìng.
1. 认识你很高兴。
   Nice to meet you.

Nǐ qù nǎr?
2. 你去哪儿？
   Where are you going?

Hǎojiǔ bú jiàn le.
3. 好久不见了。
   I haven't seen you for a long time.

Zuìjìn zěnmeyàng?
4. 最近怎么样？
   How are you getting along these days?

Hái kěyǐ.
5. 还可以。
   Not so bad.

Máng shénme ne?
6. 忙什么呢？
   What are you busy with?

D: 大卫 (*David*)   W: 王明 (*Wang Ming*)
LD: 李丹 (*Li Dan*)   LL: 老罗 (*Lao Luo*)

Dialogues

(1) 初次见面 chū cì jiànmiàn

D: 你好！ Nǐ hǎo!

W: 你好！ Nǐ hǎo!

D: 认识你很高兴。 Rènshi nǐ hěn gāoxìng.

W: 我也很高兴。 Wǒ yě hěn gāoxìng.

(2) 熟人相遇 shúrén xiāng yù

（路上偶遇。） (Lù shang ǒu yù.)

LD: 王明！ Wáng Míng!

W: 李丹！（看到李丹拿着球拍） Lǐ Dān! (kàndào Lǐ Dān názhe qiúpāi)
你去打球？ Nǐ qù dǎ qiú?

LD: 对。你去哪儿？ Duì. Nǐ qù nǎr?

W: 我去机场接朋友。 Wǒ qù jīchǎng jiē péngyou.

LD: 再见！ Zàijiàn!

W: 再见！ Zàijiàn!

(1) Meeting for the First Time

D: Hello!

W: Hello!

D: Nice to meet you.

W: Nice to meet you, too.

(2) Running into an Old Acquaintance

(meeting by chance on the way)

LD: Hello, Wang Ming.

W: Hi, Li Dan. *(seeing Li Dan holding a racket)* Going to a ball game?

LD: Yes. Where are you going?

W: I'm going to the airport to pick up a friend.

LD: Bye.

W: See you.

(3) 旧友重逢 jiùyǒu chóngféng

W: 嘿，老罗！
Hēi, Lǎo Luó!

LL: 是王明啊！好久不见了。
Shì Wáng Míng a! Hǎojiǔ bú jiàn le.

最近怎么样？
Zuìjìn zěnmeyàng?

W: 还可以。
Hái kěyǐ.

LL: 忙什么呢？
Máng shénme ne?

W: 忙工作呗。听说你去海南了，
Máng gōngzuò bei. Tīngshuō nǐ qù Hǎinán le,

什么时候回来的？
shénme shíhou huílái de?

LL: 昨天刚回来。
Zuótiān gāng huílái.

W: 出差吗？
Chūchāi ma?

LL: 不是，去旅游。
Bú shì, qù lǚyóu.

W: 好棒啊！玩儿得怎么样？
Hǎo bàng a! Wánr de zěnmeyàng?

LL: 很开心。
Hěn kāixīn.

(3) Reunion of Old Friends

W: Hi, Lao Luo.

LL: Hi, Wang Ming. I haven't seen you for a long time. How are you getting along these days?

W: Not so bad.

LL: What are you busy with?

W: Working. I hear you went to Hainan Province. When did you get back?

LL: Only yesterday.

W: On business?

LL: No, for a vacation.

W: Wonderful! How did you enjoy it?

LL: I really enjoyed it.

New Words

认识	rènshi	know
机场	jīchǎng	airport
最近	zuìjìn	recently
出差	chūchāi	on business
旅游	lǚyóu	travel
开心	kāixīn	happy

Additional Expressions

Greetings

您好!	Nín hǎo!	Hello! *(to a respected person)*
大家好!	Dàjiā hǎo!	Hello, everybody!
早上好!	Zǎoshang hǎo!	Good morning!
晚上好!	Wǎnshang hǎo!	Good evening!

Chinese Ways of Greeting

When exchanging greetings, Chinese people do not only say,"*Ni hao*!"("Hello!"). They greet each other in other ways as well; in ways that show an interest in their friends. Those greetings vary at different times and in different places.

Around lunch or dinner a Chinese person often greets an acquaintance by saying, "*Chile ma*?"("Have you had your meal?") This is only a greeting. He doesn't really want to know if the other person has eaten, nor does his greeting imply an invitation. The response to this greeting is usually, "*Chi le. Ni ne*?" ("Yes, I have. What about you?")

Some other greetings that are frequently used in Chinese are "*Ni qu nar*?" ("Where are you going?"), "*Ni gan shenme qu*?" ("What are you going there for?"), "*Ni mang shenme ne*?" ("What are you busy with?"), "*Ni zai gan shenme*?" ("What are you doing now?"), etc. These questions may be considered impolite in western countries because they seem to infringe on other people's privacy. However, a Chinese person would gladly answer them. For instance, if you meet someone in a bank, he may ask you, "*Qu qian ma?*" ("Withdrawing money?"), and you can answer, "*Dui, qu dianr qian.*" ("Yes, I'm withdrawing some money.") If you meet him in a library, he may ask, "*Jie shu ma?*" ("Hi, borrowing some books?") You can reply, "*Bu, huan ji ben shu.*" ("No, I'm returning a few books.")

2 介绍 jièshào
Introduction

Basic Sentences

7. 我姓王，叫王明。
   Wǒ xìng Wáng, jiào Wáng Míng.
   My last name is Wang. My name is Wang Ming.

8. 请问您怎么称呼？
   Qǐngwèn nín zěnme chēnghu?
   What's your name, please?

9. 您是哪国人？
   Nín shì nǎ guó rén?
   Where are you from?

10. 那位是谁？
    Nà wèi shì shéi?
    Who is she (he)?

11. 我来给你介绍一下。
    Wǒ lái gěi nǐ jièshào yíxià.
    I'd like to introduce you to...

12. 你是做什么工作的？
    Nǐ shì zuò shénme gōngzuò de?
    What do you do?

M: 马克 (*Mark*) W: 王明 (*Wang Ming*)
L: 李丹 (*Li Dan*) B: 白梅 (*Bai Mei*)

Dialogues

(1) 自我介绍 zìwǒ jièshào

W: 你好！ 我姓王， 叫王明，
Nǐ hǎo! Wǒ xìng Wáng, jiào Wáng Míng,
"明白"的明。
"míngbai" de míng.

M: 你好！ 我叫马克， 叫我小马
Nǐ hǎo! Wǒ jiào Mǎkè, jiào wǒ Xiǎo Mǎ
也行。
yě xíng.

W: 欢迎欢迎。
Huānyíng huānyíng.

M: 谢谢！
Xièxie!

(2) 询问对方 xúnwèn duìfāng

W: 您好！ 请问您怎么称呼？
Nín hǎo! Qǐngwèn nín zěnme chēnghu?

B: 我叫May, 中文名字是白梅。
Wǒ jiào May, Zhōngwén míngzi shì Bái Méi.
你呢？
Nǐ ne?

W: 我叫王明。 您是哪国人？
Wǒ jiào Wáng Míng. Nín shì nǎ guó rén?

B: 我是美国人。
Wǒ shì Měiguórén.

(1) Introducing Oneself

W: Hello! My last name is Wang. My name is Wang Ming. "Ming" as in "*mingbai*".

M: Hello! I'm Mark. You can call me Xiao Ma.

W: Welcome.

M: Thank you.

(2) Asking Someone About Something

W: Hello. What's your name, please?

B: My name is May. My Chinese name is Bai Mei, and yours?

W: I'm Wang Ming. Where are you from?

B: I'm from America.

(3) 介绍别人

M: 那位是谁？

W: 她叫李丹，是一个公司的翻译。

M: 她参加今天的宴会吗？

W: 对。哎，李丹，你来一下！

（李丹跑过来。）

W: 我来给你介绍一下。这位是李丹，我们是小学同学。

L:（对马克）你好！

W: 这位是马克。

M: 李小姐，认识你很高兴。

L: 认识你我也很高兴。你是美国人吗？

M: 不是，我是法国人，我妈妈是美国人。

L: 你是做什么工作的？

M: 我做法律方面的工作。

(3) Introducing Others

M: Who is she?

W: She's Li Dan, interpreter for a company.

M: Is she going to the banquet tonight?

W: Yes. Hey, Li Dan, come over here.

(Li Dan runs over.)

W: I'd like to introduce you to Li Dan. We were elementary school classmates.

L: *(to Mark)* Hi.

W: This is Mark.

M: Miss Li, pleased to meet you.

L: Pleased to meet you, too. Are you American?

M: No, I'm French. My mother is American.

L: What do you do?

M: I am a lawyer.

New Words

称呼	chēnghu	address
公司	gōngsī	company
翻译	fānyì	interpreter
参加	cānjiā	attend
宴会	yànhuì	banquet
法律	fǎlù	law

Additional Expressions

Professions

医生	yīshēng	doctor
律师	lǜshī	lawyer
职员	zhíyuán	staff member
商人	shāngrén	businessman
公务员	gōngwùyuán	civil servant
工程师	gōngchéngshī	engineer

TIP   *Chinese Names*

A Chinese name is made up of two parts: the family name and the given name. Most Chinese family names are monosyllabic and are represented by only one Chinese character, such as "Zhang," "Wang," "Li," "Zhao," "Liu" or "Zhou." There are a few Chinese whose family names are two syllables, that is, with two characters: "Ouyang," "Sima," "Shangguan," etc.

In a Chinese name the family name precedes the first name. For example, in "Zhang Ping" and "Li Aihua," "Zhang" and "Li" are family names. As for the first name, it can either be monosyllabic or disyllabic. "Wang Yu," "Zhou Lihong" and "Ouyang Baixue" are examples of full Chinese names. Children usually have pet names. Duplication or putting "Xiao" before the name are common ways to give a pet name to a child. "Mingming," "Lili," "Xiaoxue" and "Xiaoyu" are cases in point. This practice is a way that parents express their love for their children.

NOTE

3 xúnwèn
询 问
Inquiry

Basic Sentences

13. Néng rènshi yíxià ma?
    能认识一下吗?
    Can I introduce myself?

14. Nǐ zài nǎr gōngzuò?
    你在哪儿工作?
    Where do you work?

15. Nǐ xǐhuan yùndòng ma?
    你喜欢运动吗?
    Do you like sports?

16. Gǎitiān wǒmen yìqǐ wánr ba!
    改天我们一起玩儿吧!
    Let's play together someday.

17. Nín xūyào shénme fúwù?
    您需要什么服务?
    Can I help you?

18. Wǒ xiǎng huàn diǎnr rénmínbì.
    我想换点儿人民币。
    I'd like to change some renminbi.

M: 马 克 (*Mark*)   W: 王 明 (*Wang Ming*)
A: 服务员 (*Attendant*)   B: 毕大伟 (*Bi dawei*)

Dialogues

zài sīrén wǎnhuì shang
(1) 在私人晚会上

W: Néng rènshi yíxià ma? Wǒ jiào Wáng Míng,
能认识一下吗？我叫王明，
nǐ ne?
你呢？

B: Wǒ jiào Bì Dàwěi. Hěn gāoxìng rènshi nǐ.
我叫毕大伟。很高兴认识你。

W: Nǐ shì zuò shénme gōngzuò de?
你是做什么工作的？

B: Wǒ zài yì jiā guójì màoyì gōngsī gōngzuò.
我在一家国际贸易公司工作。
Nǐ zài nǎr gōngzuò?
你在哪儿工作？

W: Wǒ zài yínháng gōngzuò. Nǐ xǐhuan yùndòng ma?
我在银行工作。你喜欢运动吗？

B: Duì. Wǒ jīngcháng dǎ wǎngqiú, yě xǐhuan
对。我经常打网球，也喜欢
kàn zúqiú.
看足球。

W: Wǒ yě xǐhuan dǎ wǎngqiú. Gǎitiān wǒmen
我也喜欢打网球。改天我们
yìqǐ wánr ba!
一起玩儿吧！

B: Hǎo a!
好啊！

(1) At a Private Party

W: Can I introduce myself? I'm Wang Ming, and you?

B: I'm Bi Dawei. Pleased to meet you.

W: What do you do?

B: I'm with a company in international trade. Where do you work?

W: I work at a bank. Do you like sports?

B: Yes, I play tennis quite often and like to watch soccer games.

W: I also like to play tennis. Let's play together someday.

B: Great.

（2）在酒店兑换外币

A：您好！您需要什么**服务**？

M：我想换点儿人民币。

A：您想换多少钱？

M：2 000块人民币。我换欧元。

A：请稍等，我查一下现在的**比价**。（用电脑查询后）现在人民币和欧元的**汇率**是10比1。所以，是200欧元。

M：对不起，请您再说一遍，我没听清楚。

A：人民币和欧元的汇率是10比1，您要付200欧元。

M：（拿出钱）给您。

A：好。这是您的人民币，一共2 000元。您数一下。

M：（数完钱后）好的，没问题。

(2) Exchanging Foreign Currency in a Hotel

A: Hello, can I help you?

M: I'd like to change some renminbi.

A: How much would you like to change?

M: 2,000 yuan. I want to change from euros.

A: Just a minute. Let me check the present exchange rate. *(checking in the computer)* Now the exchange rate between renminbi and euro is 10 to 1. So 200 euros.

M: Sorry. Can you say it again? I didn't hear you very clearly.

A: The exchange rate between renminbi and euro is 10 to 1, so you need to pay me 200 euros.

M: *(taking out his money)* Here you are.

A: Good. Here is your renminbi, 2,000 yuan in all. Would you please check it?

M: *(counting his money)* Excellent, there's no problem.

New Words

国际	guójì	international
贸易	màoyì	trade
改天	gǎitiān	some other day
服务	fúwù	service
比价	bǐjià	price comparison
汇率	huìlǜ	exchange rate

Additional Expressions

Time

年	nián	year
月	yuè	month
星期	xīngqī	week
周	zhōu	week
天	tiān	day
小时	xiǎoshí	hour
分钟	fēnzhōng	minute
秒	miǎo	second

TIP

Currency

USD	美元	měiyuán
EUR	欧元	ōuyuán
GBP	英镑	yīngbàng
JPY	日元	rìyuán
CHF	瑞士法郎	Ruìshì fǎláng
CAD	加拿大元（加元）	Jiānádà yuán (jiāyuán)
HKD	港币	gǎngbì
NZD	新西兰元	Xīnxīlán yuán
KRW	韩国元（韩元）	Hánguó yuán (hányuán)
AUD	澳大利亚元（澳元）	Àodàlìyà yuán (àoyuán)
PHP	菲律宾比索	Fēilùbīn bǐsuǒ
SGD	新加坡元	Xīnjiāpō yuán
THB	泰国铢	Tàiguó zhū
RUB	俄罗斯卢布	Éluósī lúbù
DEM	德国马克	Déguó mǎkè

NOTE

4 邀请和约定
yāoqǐng hé yuēdìng
Invitations and Appointments

Basic Sentences

19. 明天晚上有空儿吗？
    Míngtiān wǎnshang yǒu kòngr ma?
    Are you free tomorrow evening?

20. 你有什么事儿吗？
    Nǐ yǒu shénme shìr ma?
    What can I do for you?

21. 你几点合适？
    Nǐ jǐ diǎn héshì?
    What time will suit you?

22. 不见不散。
    Bújiàn-búsàn.
    I'll see you there.

23. 你还有别的安排吗？
    Nǐ hái yǒu bié de ānpái ma?
    Do you have other plans?

24. 没问题，来得及。
    Méi wèntí, láidejí.
    No problem. You'll have enough time.

M: 马 克 (*Mark*)   W: 王 明 (*Wang Ming*)
B: 白 梅 (*Bai Mei*)

Dialogues

(1) yāoqǐng biérén yìqǐ chīfàn
邀请别人一起吃饭

W: Bái Méi, míngtiān wǎnshang yǒu kòngr ma?
白梅，明天晚上有空儿吗？

B: Bàoqiàn, míngtiān wǎnshang wǒ yǒu kè. Nǐ yǒu shénme shìr ma?
抱歉，明天晚上我有课。你有什么事儿吗？

W: Wǒ xiǎng qǐng nǐ hé jǐ gè péngyou yìqǐ chī wǎnfàn.
我想请你和几个朋友一起吃晚饭。

B: Hòutiān wǎnshang xíng ma?
后天晚上行吗？

W: Xíng a. Nǐ jǐ diǎn héshì?
行啊。你几点合适？

B: Liù diǎn bàn zěnmeyàng?
6点半怎么样？

W: Nà jiù liù diǎn bàn.
那就6点半。

B: Zài shénme dìfang?
在什么地方？

W: Quánjùdé.
全聚德。

B: Nǎ jiā Quánjùdé?
哪家全聚德？

W: Qiánmén de nà yì jiā. Wǒmen zài ménkǒu jiàn.
前门的那一家。我们在门口见。

B: Hǎo, bújiàn-búsàn!
好，不见不散！

W: Bújiàn-búsàn!
不见不散！

(1) Inviting People for a Meal

W: Bai Mei, are you free tomorrow evening?

B: I'm sorry I have classes tomorrow evening. What can I do for you?

W: I'd like to invite you and a few friends to dinner.

B: Will the evening of the day after tomorrow be all right?

W: That's good. What time will suit you?

B: What about half past six?

W: Then let's make it six thirty.

B: Where?

W: Quanjude.

B: Which Quanjude?

W: The one at Qianmen. We'll meet at the gate.

B: Good, I'll see you there.

W: I'll see you there, too.

(2) 邀请朋友看京剧
yāoqǐng péngyou kàn jīngjù

W: 马克,我有两张京剧票,星期五晚上的,我们一起去看吧。
Mǎkè, wǒ yǒu liǎng zhāng jīngjù piào, xīngqīwǔ wǎnshang de, wǒmen yìqǐ qù kàn ba.

M: 太好啦!在哪儿?
Tài hǎo la! Zài nǎr?

W: 国家大剧院。
Guójiā Dà Jùyuàn.

M: 几点?
Jǐ diǎn?

W: 星期五晚上7点半。
Xīngqīwǔ wǎnshang qī diǎn bàn.

M: 大概演多长时间?
Dàgài yǎn duōcháng shíjiān?

W: 大概一个半小时。你还有别的安排吗?
Dàgài yí gè bàn xiǎoshí. Nǐ hái yǒu bié de ānpái ma?

M: 我11点还有一个约会。
Wǒ shíyī diǎn hái yǒu yí gè yuēhuì.

W: 没问题,来得及。我6点半到你那儿接你。晚饭就吃麦当劳吧。
Méi wèntí, láidejí. Wǒ liù diǎn bàn dào nǐ nàr jiē nǐ. Wǎnfàn jiù chī Màidāngláo ba.

M: 好,星期五见!
Hǎo, xīngqīwǔ jiàn!

(2) Inviting Friends to a Beijing Opera Show

W: Mark, I've got two Beijing Opera tickets for Friday evening. We can go together and see it.

M: Excellent. Where?

W: The National Theater.

M: What time?

W: Friday evening at half past seven.

M: About how long will the show last?

W: About one and a half hours. Do you have other plans?

M: Yes, I have an appointment at eleven o'clock.

W: No problem. You'll have enough time. I'll pick you up at half past six. Let's have McDonald's for supper.

M: OK, see you Friday.

New Words

合适	héshì	suit
京剧	jīngjù	Beijing Opera
安排	ānpái	arrangement
约会	yuēhuì	appointment

Additional Expressions

Common Chain Restaurants

肯德基	Kěndéjī	Kentucky Fried Chicken
赛百味	Sàibǎiwèi	Subway
必胜客	Bìshèngkè	Pizza Hut
棒约翰	Bàngyuēhàn	Papa John
星巴克	Xīngbākè	Starbucks
吉野家	Jíyějiā	Yoshinoya
真功夫	Zhēngōngfu	Kungfu
面爱面	Miàn'àimiàn	Kyo-nichi Restaurant
呷哺呷哺	Xiābǔ Xiābǔ	Xiabu Xiabu

Beijing Opera

Beijing Opera, a quintessential part of Chinese culture, has a history of over two hundred years. With many operas, stage artists, opera troupes and fans, Beijing Opera is the most influential among the different types of Chinese traditional operas.

Beijing Opera is a type of comprehensive performing art that combines singing, recitation, performing, acrobatic martial arts skills and dancing. Its stylized movements are effective for telling stories, portraying different characters and expressing happiness, anger, grief, cheerfulness, surprise, terror and sorrow.

Beijing Opera roles are classified into four major role types according to the age and personality of the characters: *Sheng* (male roles), *Dan* (female roles), *Jing* (painted face roles) and *Chou* (clowns).

Beijing Opera now boasts more than 5,800 operas, most of which are traditional operas. The most popular ones are *Jiangxianghe* (*The General and the Minister Are Reconciled*), *Qunyinghui* (*Gathering of Heroes*), *Kongchengji* (*Empty City Ruse*), *Guifei Zuijiu* (*The*

Drunken Beauty), *Sanchakou* (*The Crossroads*), *Shi Yuzhuo* (*Picking up the Jade Bracelet*) and *Dayushajia* (*The Fisherman's Revenge*).

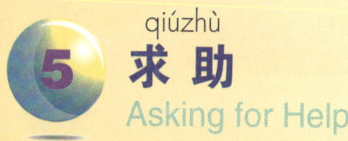

5 求助 qiúzhù
Asking for Help

Basic Sentences

25. Dǎchē qù háishi zuò gōnggòng qìchē qù?
    打车去还是坐公共汽车去？
    Should I go there by taxi or by bus?

26. Zěnme zǒu?
    怎么走？
    How should I go?

27. Chūmén xiàng yòu guǎi, yìzhí wǎng qián zǒu.
    出门向右拐，一直往前走。
    Turn right at the gate and then go straight ahead.

28. Bié zháojí, shénme shíhou diū de?
    别着急，什么时候丢的？
    Don't worry. When did you lose it?

29. Shénmeyàng de qiánbāo?
    什么样的钱包？
    What kind of a wallet is it?

30. Qǐng nín dēngjì yíxià.
    请您登记一下。
    Please fill out this form.

B: 白 梅 (*Bai Mei*)　　P: 警 察 (*Policeman*)
W: 王 明 (*Wang Ming*)　M: 马 克 (*Mark*)

Dialogues

(1) 问路 wèn lù

B: 我想去超市发买点东西，打车去还是坐公共汽车去？
Wǒ xiǎng qù Chāoshìfā mǎi diǎn dōngxi, dǎ chē qù háishi zuò gōnggòng qìchē qù?

W: 超市发太远了。附近有一家新开的大超市，离这儿很近，不用坐车，走过去就行了。
Chāoshìfā tài yuǎn le. Fùjìn yǒu yì jiā xīn kāi de dà chāoshì, lí zhèr hěn jìn, bú yòng zuò chē, zǒu guòqù jiù xíng le.

B: 怎么走？
Zěnme zǒu?

W: 出门向右拐，一直往前走，大概走10分钟就到了，在马路的左边。
Chū mén xiàng yòu guǎi, yìzhí wǎng qián zǒu, dàgài zǒu shí fēnzhōng jiù dào le, zài mǎlù de zuǒbian.

(2) 向警察报案 xiàng jǐngchá bào'àn

P: 您好！发生什么事儿了？
Nín hǎo! Fāshēng shénme shìr le?

M: 警察先生，我的钱包丢了！
Jǐngchá xiānsheng, wǒ de qiánbāo diū le!

P: 别着急，什么时候丢的？
Bié zháojí, shénme shíhou diū de?

(1) Asking the Way

B: I'd like to go to Chaoshifa Supermarket. Should I go there by taxi or by bus?

W: It is so far to Chaoshifa. There's a newly opened supermarket in the neighborhood. It's not far away, so you don't need to go by bus. It's within walking distance.

B: How should I go?

W: Turn right at the gate and then go straight ahead. It's about a ten minute walk. It's on your left-hand side.

(2) Reporting to the Police

P: Hello. What happened?

M: Sir, I've lost my wallet!

P: Don't worry. When did you lose it?

M: 半个小时以前。

P: 在哪儿丢的?

M: 应该是我们附近的超市。

P: 什么样的钱包?

M: 黑色的,皮的。

P: 里面都有什么东西?

M: 有欧元和人民币,大概200多欧元和1000元左右人民币。还有几张卡。

P: 请您登记一下,填上您的姓名、地址和联系方式。有消息我们就通知您。

M: 能告诉我你们的电话吗?

P: 我给你写下来吧。您可以找我,我姓刘,刘立华。

M: Half an hour ago.

P: Where did you lose it?

M: I believe in the supermarket in our neighborhood.

P: What kind of a wallet is it?

M: Black, made of leather.

P: What's inside?

M: Some euros and renminbi; more than 200 euros and about 1,000 renminbi, and a few cards as well.

P: Please fill out this form. Write down your name, address and contact information. We'll inform you if there are any developments.

M: Could you tell me your telephone number?

P: Let me write it down for you. You can ask for me. My name is Liu Lihua.

New Words

警察	jǐngchá	policeman
登记	dēngjì	register
填	tián	fill in (a form)
联系方式	liánxì fāngshì	way of contact
消息	xiāoxi	news; information
通知	tōngzhī	inform

Additional Expressions

Traffic

向/往左转	xiàng/wǎng zuǒ zhuǎn	turn left
斑马线	bānmǎxiàn	pedestrian crosswalk
人行道	rénxíngdào	sidewalk
自行车道	zìxíngchēdào	bicycle lane
十字路口	shízì lùkǒu	intersection
丁字路口	dīngzì lùkǒu	T-shaped intersection
红绿灯	hónglǜdēng	traffic light
交通警察	jiāotōng jǐngchá	traffic police

TIP

Telephone Numbers for Assistance in China

Name of Service	Telephone Number	Time	Charge
crime report	110	24 hours	free
fire department	119	24 hours	free
first-aid station	120/999	24 hours	free
telephone information	114	24 hours	local call rate
time information	12117	24 hours	local call rate
weather forecast	12121	24 hours	local call rate
traffic accident report	122	24 hours	free
Beijing postal service	11185	24 hours	free

NOTE

kànbìng
看病
Seeing a Doctor

Basic Sentences

Nǐ hǎo, nǐ nǎr bù shūfu?
31. 你好，你哪儿不舒服？
Hello, what seems to be bothering you?

Wǒ tóu téng, késou, shuì bu hǎo jiào, sǎngzi yě bù shūfu.
32. 我头疼，咳嗽，睡不好觉，嗓子也不舒服。
I have a headache, cough, insomnia and a sore throat as well.

Liáng yíxià tǐwēn ba.
33. 量一下体温吧。
Let me take your temperature.

Nín gěi wǒ kāi xiē yào ba.
34. 您给我开些药吧。
Please prescribe some medicine for me.

Zhè yào zěnme chī?
35. 这药怎么吃？
How do I take this medicine?

Duō hē shuǐ, duō xiūxi.
36. 多喝水，多休息。
You need to drink plenty of water and rest for a few days.

B: 白 梅（*Bai Mei*）   D: 医 生（*Doctor*）
S: 售货员（*Salesman*）   M: 马 克（*Mark*）

Dialogues

(1) 在医院 zài yīyuàn

D: 你好，你哪儿不舒服？
Nǐ hǎo, nǐ nǎr bù shūfu?

M: 我头疼，咳嗽，睡不好觉，嗓子也不舒服。可能感冒了。
Wǒ tóu téng, késou, shuì bu hǎo jiào, sǎngzi yě bù shūfu. Kěnéng gǎnmào le.

D: 让我检查一下。来，张口，说"啊——"，嗓子发炎了。量一下体温吧。（量完后）你有点儿发烧。
Ràng wǒ jiǎnchá yíxià. Lái, zhāngkǒu, shuō "ā——", sǎngzi fāyán le. Liáng yíxià tǐwēn ba. (liángwán hòu) Nǐ yǒu diǎnr fāshāo.

M: 您给我开些药吧。
Nín gěi wǒ kāi xiē yào ba.

D: 你还得查一下血，看看是病毒性感冒还是细菌性感冒。请拿这个单子先划价再查血。
Nǐ hái děi chá yíxià xiě, kànkan shì bìngdúxìng gǎnmào háishi xìjūnxìng gǎnmào. Qǐng ná zhège dānzi xiān huàjià zài chá xiě.

M: 这么复杂啊！
Zhème fùzá a!

D: 最近流行的感冒比较特别，还是要对症下药。
Zuìjìn liúxíng de gǎnmào bǐjiào tèbié, háishi yào duìzhèng-xiàyào.

(1) Seeing a Doctor

D: Hello, what seems to be bothering you?

M: I have a headache, cough, insomnia and a sore throat as well. I might have caught a cold.

D: Let me check. Open your mouth and say "Ah—." Your throat is inflamed. Let me take your temperature. *(after taking the temperature)* You have a fever.

M: Please prescribe some medicine for me.

D: You need to have a blood test to find out if your cold was caused by a virus or bacteria. Please take this referral and pay for the procedure before taking your blood test.

M: It's so complicated.

D: Colds have been unusually rampant recently and we should apply the right medicine for an illness.

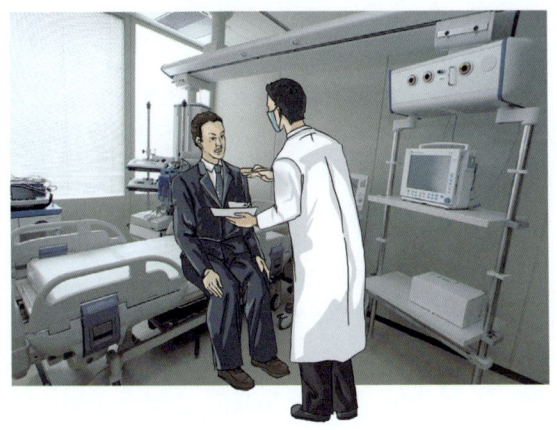

(Mǎkè cháwán xiě hòu huílái.)
(马克查完血后回来。)

D:(xiě yàofāng)Hǎo de. Qǐng ná zhè zhāng yàofāng dào yàofáng ná yào.
D:(写药方)好的。请拿这张药方到药房拿药。

(2) 在药店买药

B: Shīfu, wǒ xiǎng mǎi diǎnr gǎnmàoyào.
B: 师傅，我想买点儿感冒药。

S: Gǎnmào duō cháng shíjiān le?
S: 感冒多长时间了？

B: Jiù shì jīntiān zǎoshang qǐlái gǎnjué bù shūfu.
B: 就是今天早上起来感觉不舒服。

S: Nín kěyǐ shìshi zhège, zhè shì zhōngchéngyào, zhì gǎnmào hěn yǒuxiào.
S: 您可以试试这个，这是中成药，治感冒很有效。

B: Zhè yào zěnme chī?
B: 这药怎么吃？

S: Měi tiān liǎng cì, yí cì yí dài, yòng wēnkāishuǐ chōngfú. Hái yào duō hē shuǐ, duō xiūxi, zhǐyào bù fāshāo, hěn kuài jiù huì hǎo de.
S: 每天两次，一次一袋，用温开水冲服。还要多喝水，多休息，只要不发烧，很快就会好的。

(Mark returns after the blood test.)

D: *(writing the prescription)* OK. Take this prescription and get your medicine at the pharmacy.

(2) At the Pharmacy

B: Hello, I'd like to buy some cold medicine.

S: How long have you had a cold?

B: I wasn't feeling very well when I got up this morning.

S: You can try this. It's Chinese patent medicine prepared by a pharmacy, and very effeective for colds.

B: How do I take this medicine?

S: Each time take one small bag, twice a day. Dissolve the medicine in hot water before taking it. You need to drink plenty of water and rest for a few days. As long as you have no fever, you'll recover soon.

New Words

发炎	fāyán	inflammation
病毒	bìngdú	virus
细菌	xìjūn	bacteria
划价	huàjià	(of hospital pharmacy) write down the amount to be paid on the prescription
复杂	fùzá	complicated
对症下药	duìzhèng-xiàyào	apply a right medicine for an illness
药方	yàofāng	prescription
有效	yǒuxiào	effective

Additional Expressions

Parts of Body

耳朵	ěrduo	ear
眼睛	yǎnjing	eye
鼻子	bízi	nose
嘴	zuǐ	mouth
牙齿	yáchǐ	tooth
头	tóu	head
手	shǒu	hand

脚	jiǎo	foot
胳膊	gēbo	arm
腿	tuǐ	leg
肚子	dùzi	belly
腰	yāo	waist
背	bèi	back
心脏	xīnzàng	heart

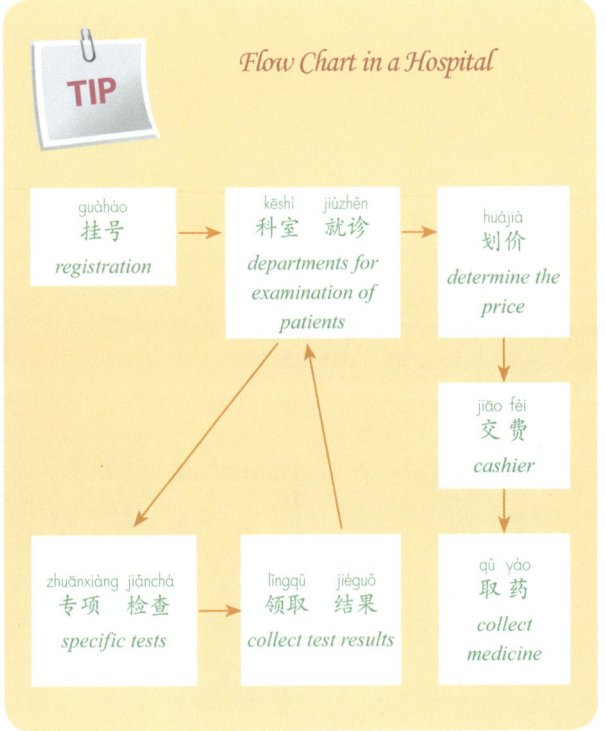

NOTE

7 感谢和道歉
gǎnxiè hé dàoqiàn
Thanks and Apology

Basic Sentences

37. Nǐ tài kèqi le!
你太客气了!
You are so kind.

38. Nǐmen yě gěile wǒ hěn duō bāngzhù.
你们也给了我很多帮助。
You've given me a lot of help as well.

39. Wǒ kěyǐ dǎkāi kànkan ma?
我可以打开看看吗?
Can I open it and have a look?

40. Nǐ xǐhuan jiù hǎo.
你喜欢就好。
I'm glad you like them.

41. Duìbuqǐ, wǒ láiwǎn le. Děngjí le ba?
对不起,我来晚了。等急了吧?
Sorry, I'm late. You must have been worried.

42. Wǒ zuò dìtiě lái jiù hǎo le.
我坐地铁来就好了。
I should have come by subway.

B: 白 梅 (*Bai Mei*)   M: 马 克 (*Mark*)
W: 王 明 (*Wang Ming*)

Dialogues

(1) dédào lǐwù
    得到礼物

W: Bái Méi, zhè shì wǒ sòng gěi nǐ de yí gè xiǎo lǐwù.
   白梅，这是我送给你的一个小礼物。

B: (yǒudiǎnr bùjiě) Sòng gěi wǒ de lǐwù?
   (有点儿不解) 送给我的礼物？

W: Nǐ jiāo wǒ mèimei Yīngyǔ, hái bāng wǒ fānyìle bù shǎo zīliào, wǒmen dōu fēicháng gǎnxiè nǐ.
   你教我妹妹英语，还帮我翻译了不少资料，我们都非常感谢你。

B: Nǐ tài kèqi le! Nǐmen yě gěile wǒ hěn duō bāngzhù.
   你太客气了！你们也给了我很多帮助。

W: Zhè shì wǒ mèimei tiāo de.
   这是我妹妹挑的。

B: Wǒ kěyǐ dǎkāi kànkan ma?
   我可以打开看看吗？

W: Dāngrán, xīwàng nǐ xǐhuan.
   当然，希望你喜欢。

B: Zhè bú shì Zhōngguó de jiǎnzhǐ ma? "Lǎoshǔ Jiànǚ", wǒ tīngshuōguo zhège gùshi.
   这不是中国的剪纸吗？"老鼠嫁女"，我听说过这个故事。

(1) Accepting a Gift

W: Bai Mei, I have a little gift for you.

B: *(bewildered)* A gift for me?

W: You've been teaching my younger sister English and have helped me translate a lot of material as well. We both feel very grateful.

B: You are so kind. You've given me a lot of help as well.

W: My younger sister chose it.

B: Can I open it and have a look?

W: Sure. Hope you like it.

B: It's Chinese papercutting, isn't it? "*The Mouse Marries Its Daughter.*" I've heard of the story.

W: 这是陕西的剪纸。你喜欢就好。

B: 我太喜欢了！谢谢你和你妹妹。
她很**聪明**，英语**进步**很大。

(2) 看演出迟到

M: 对不起，我来晚了。等急了吧？

W: 没关系。我也是刚到。

M: 公司临时有事儿，又碰上**堵车**。

W: 上下班时间嘛，免不了。

M: 我坐地铁来就好了。

W: 地铁比较快，但现在也会很**挤**。

M: 时间还来得及吗？

W: 没问题。7点半开演，还有10分钟。

M: 我们进去吧。

W: This is Shaanxi style paper-cut. I'm glad you like it.

B: I really like it! Thank you, and your sister as well. She's very clever and has made great progress in English.

(2) Arriving Late to a Show

M: Sorry I'm late. You must have been worried.

W: It's all right. I've also just arrived.

M: I had something to attend to at my company at the last minute, and then there was a traffic jam.

W: It's unavoidable during the rush hour.

M: I should have come by subway.

W: It's faster by subway, but probably also very crowded at this time.

M: Have we got enough time?

W: No problem. The show starts at half past seven. We still have ten minutes.

M: Let's go in.

New Words

翻译	fānyì	translate
资料	zīliào	data; material
剪纸	jiǎnzhǐ	paper-cut
故事	gùshi	story
聪明	cōngmíng	clever
进步	jìnbù	progress
堵车	dǔchē	traffic jam
挤	jǐ	crowded

Additional Expressions

Gratitude and Apology

谢谢你的好意。
Xièxie nǐ de hǎoyì.
Thank you for your kindness.

真不知该怎么感谢你!
Zhēn bùzhī gāi zěnme gǎnxiè nǐ!
I really don't know how to thank you!

多亏你的帮助!
Duōkuī nǐ de bāngzhù!
Thanks to your help!

给你添麻烦了。
Gěi nǐ tiān máfan le.
I'm sorry to bother you.

耽误你时间了。
Dānwù nǐ shíjiān le.
I'm sorry to waste your time.

Giving Presents in China

Chinese people, when invited to a family dinner, usually bring some presents with them, such as a bouquet of flowers, fruit or local products unique to their area. If there are children in the family, toys, sweets and chocolates are good gifts. Health care products will be suitable gifts if there are elderly people in the family. When going to a wedding party, people may choose artwork, pratical items or just cash gifts. During festivals, tea, sweets, cigarettes and wine are usually people's gift choices.

However, there are a few things to be careful of when giving gifts in China. There is a taboo on giving an old person a clock as gift, because the Chinese words for "giving a clock" sounds like the phrase "attending upon a dying relative". Also due to homophone issues, pears and umbrellas must not be given to newly married couple as they are often associated with divorce. In addition, it is inappropriate to give health care products to healthy people or to give personal things to friends of the opposite sex.

For foreigners going to China, a special product unique to their home country would be an approprite gift. Coffee, tea, spices, wine, perfume and cosmetics, as well as health care products such as Centrum and cod liver oil, are very popular in China.

NOTE

8 chēngzàn
称 赞
Compliments

Basic Sentences

Wǒ néng kàn yíxià rìchéng ma?
37. 我能看一下日程吗？
Can I have a look at your schedule?

Nǐmen lǎobǎn hěn nénggàn a!
38. 你们老板很能干啊！
Your boss is very competent.

Ānpái hěn hélǐ, jiàqián yě bǐjiào gōngdào.
39. 安排很合理，价钱也比较公道。
The arrangements are good and the price is also reasonable.

Nǐ chuān de zhēn piàoliang!
40. 你穿得真漂亮！
You really look great in that dress.

Wǒ chàdiǎnr rèn bu chūlái le!
41. 我差点儿认不出来了！
I hardly recognized you.

Nǐ jīntiān yě hěn shuài ma!
42. 你今天也很帅嘛！
You also look handsome today.

A: 服务员（*Attendant*）　M: 马　克（*Mark*）
W: 王安安（*Wang An'an*）

Dialogues

(1) 称赞旅行安排 chēngzàn lǚxíng ānpái

M: 您好！我想问问你们的"北京三日游"。我能看一下日程吗？

A: 给您，这是**具体**的活动安排。中英文都有。

M: 有四合院啊！我一直想参观四合院，了解一下老北京的情况。哦，还有香山！我早就听说过。我喜欢爬山。这个价格**包括**哪些费用？

A: 餐费、住宿费、门票全部包括在里面，不另外收取其他费用。

(1) Discussing Travel Arrangements

M: I'd like to get some information about your "Three-day tour of Beijing." Can I have a look at the schedule?

A: Here it is. It has the detailed arrangements. It's in both Chinese and English.

M: It includes a vistit to a *siheyuan (quadrangle dwelling)*. I have been looking forward to visiting a *siheyuan* and learning about old Beijing. Oh, it also has the Fragrant Hills! I have been hearing about that for some time now. I like climbing mountains. What does the price include?

A: Meals, accommodation and admission fees are all included. There are no additional charges.

M: 很好。在哪里用餐?

A: 我们会去东来顺吃火锅,去西贝莜面村品尝中国西北风味,还会让大家吃到地道的老北京炸酱面。我们去的都是有地方特色的餐馆。

M: 你们老板很**能干**啊!安排很**合理**,价钱也比较**公道**。我看看我的时间,然后再跟你们联系。

(2) 称赞 服装

M: 嘿,安安!你去哪儿?

W: 今天有个宴会。

M: Very good. Where do we have our meals?

A: We'll have hot pot at "Dong Lai Shun" (*a time-honored brand for hot pot*) and taste Chinese Northwestern regional cuisine at "Xibei Youmian Cun" (*a restaurant famous for oat noodles*). We'll also provide an opportunity for you to eat authentic old Beijing noodles (*a kind of fried noodle with soy bean paste*). All the restaurants where we go to eat are known for their regional distinctiveness.

M: Your boss is very competent. The arrangements are good and the price is also reasonable. I'll check my schedule before I call you again.

(2) Giving Compliments on Dress

M: Hey, An'an! Where are you going?

W: There's a banquet today.

M: 你穿得真漂亮！这件旗袍一穿，我差点儿认不出来了！

W: 你过奖了！我昨天刚取回来。

M: 在哪儿买的？我也想给我女朋友买一件。

W: 在王府井的一个旗袍店，那里有现成的，也可以订做，他们的手艺很好。

M: 太好了！我一定带她去看看。

W: 你今天也很帅嘛！和女朋友约会吧？

M: 没错！我得赶紧走了。

W: 快去吧。别迟到！

M: You really look great in that dress. I hardly recognized you in that cheongsam *(a kind of traditional Chinese dress for women)*.

W: Thank you. I picked it up only yesterday.

M: Where did you buy it? I'd also like to buy one for my girlfriend.

W: In a cheongsam shop in Wangfujing Avenue. They are ready-made ones. You can also have them made to order. Their craftsmanship is excellent.

M: Wonderful. I'll certainly take her there to have a look.

W: You also look handsome today. You have a date with your girlfriend, don't you?

M: Yes, I'm in a hurry, and I have to go now.

W: Go ahead. Don't be late.

Cheongsam

New Words

具体	jùtǐ	specific
包括	bāokuò	include
能干	nénggàn	competent
合理	hélǐ	reasonable
公道	gōngdào	fair
现成	xiànchéng	ready-made
手艺	shǒuyì	craftsmanship

Additional Expressions

Compliments

很有魅力。	Hěn yǒu mèilì.	Very charming.
真牛!	Zhēn niú!	Great!
棒极了!	Bàng jí le!	Wonderful!
真了不起!		
	Zhēn liǎobuqǐ!	
	You're really something!	
谁都比不上你。		
	Shéi dōu bǐ bu shàng nǐ.	
	No one can be better than you.	

Chinese Response to Praise

Chinese people have always considered modesty to be a virtue. When praised, one usually tries to be modest even if he really deserves the praise, or else he may look conceited in the eyes of others. Normally in such cases one may reply by saying, "That's not true. I'm far behind you." "You've done better than I." "Not so bad." "You are flattering me." "Thank you, so do you." etc.

Some young people, due to the influence of western culture, often say, "Thank you" or "I'm very grateful" as well to respond to praise, especially to compliments from casual friends or on informal occasions. When recommending themselves either in an interview or in a lecture, young people also like to mention their special skills and merits matter-of-factly. However, when good friends get together, they brag.

NOTE

9 zhùhè
祝贺
Congratulations

> **Basic Sentences**

49. Zhù nǐ shēngrì kuàilè!
    祝你生日快乐！
    Happy birthday!

50. Ràng wǒmen wèi xīnláng xīnniáng de xìngfú gānbēi!
    让我们为新郎新娘的幸福干杯！
    Let's toast to the happiness of the bride and bridegroom!

51. Zhù nǐmen héhé-měiměi, ēn'ēn-ài'ài, báitóu-dàolǎo!
    祝你们和和美美，恩恩爱爱，白头到老！
    Best wishes to the two of you for happiness and conjugal love throughout your whole life!

52. Wǒmen yě jìng nǐ yì bēi.
    我们也敬你一杯。
    Here's to you.

53. Nǐ zài Zhōngguó de gōngzuò yě hěn shùnlì ma!
    你在中国的工作也很顺利嘛！
    You are also very successful in your business in China.

54. Gǎirì wǒmen yìqǐ qìngzhù yíxià ba.
    改日我们一起庆祝一下吧。
    Let's celebrate it together some other time.

M: 马 克（*Mark*） W: 王安安（*Wang An'an*）
G: 客人们（*Guests*） Y: 叶 总（*Mr. Ye*）
B: 新郎、新娘（*Bride and Bridegroom*）

Dialogues

(1) 在生日会上
zài shēngrìhuì shang

M: 安安，祝你生日快乐！这是我和女朋友送给你的生日礼物。
Ān'ān, zhù nǐ shēngrì kuàilè! Zhè shì wǒ hé nǚpéngyou sòng gěi nǐ de shēngrì lǐwù.

W: 啊，这么大的米老鼠！太可爱了！
Ā, zhème dà de mǐlǎoshǔ! Tài kě'ài le!

M: 你是属鼠的嘛。
Nǐ shì shǔ shǔ de ma.

W: 你们想得真周到！谢谢！
Nǐmen xiǎng de zhēn zhōudào! Xièxie!

M: 来，我们一起给安安唱生日快乐歌吧。
Lái, wǒmen yìqǐ gěi Ān'ān chàng Shēngrì Kuàilè gē ba.

(2) 在婚礼上
zài hūnlǐ shang

M: 你们让我说两句，我就说两句。
Nǐmen ràng wǒ shuō liǎng jù, wǒ jiù shuō liǎng jù.

今天是个好日子，让我们为新郎新娘的幸福干杯！
Jīntiān shì gè hǎo rìzi, ràng wǒmen wèi xīnláng xīnniáng de xìngfú gānbēi!

(1) At a Birthday Party

M: An'an, happy birthday! This is me and my girlfriend's gift for your birthday.

W: Oh, such a big Mickey Mouse. It's so lovely!

M: You were born in the year of Rat.

W: You are really considerate! Thank you!

M: Come on, Let's sing "*Happy Birthday*" to An'an.

(2) At a Wedding

M: I'll say a few words, as you wanted me to. Today is a special day. Let's toast to the happiness of the bride and bridegroom.

G: Gānbēi!
干杯！

M: Nǐmen shì tiānshēng de yí duìr, zhù nǐmen héhé-měiměi, ēn'ēn-ài'ài, báitóu-dàolǎo!
你们是天生的一对儿，祝你们和和美美，恩恩爱爱，白头到老！

B: Xièxie! Wǒmen yě jìng nǐ yì bēi.
谢谢！我们也敬你一杯。

(3) 祝贺事情取得成功
zhùhè shìqing qǔdé chénggōng

M: Yèzǒng, tīngshuō nín nǚ'ér kǎoshàng Běidà le, tā hěn yōuxiù a! Zhùhè nín!
叶总，听说您女儿考上北大了，她很优秀啊！祝贺您！

Y: Xièxie, xièxie! Nǐ zài Zhōngguó de gōngzuò yě hěn shùnlì ma!
谢谢，谢谢！你在中国的工作也很顺利嘛！

M: Hái búcuò, hái děi gǎnxiè nín de bāngzhù.
还不错，还得感谢您的帮助。

Gǎirì wǒmen yìqǐ qìngzhù yíxià ba.
改日我们一起庆祝一下吧。

Y: Hǎo, yìyán-wéidìng!
好，一言为定！

B: Cheers!

M: You are a heavenly pair. Best wishes to the two of you for happiness and conjugal love throughout your whole life!

B: Thanks! Here's to you.

(3) Congratulating Someone on His/Her Success

M: Mr. Ye, I heard your daughter has been admitted to Peking University. She's so outstanding! Congratulations!

Y: Thank you, thank you! You are also very successful in your business in China.

M: Not so bad. I should thank you for your help. Let's celebrate it together some other time.

Y: Good. We'll do that!

New Words

属	shǔ	be born in the year of (Chinese zodiac)
周到	zhōudào	considerate
新郎	xīnláng	bridegroom
新娘	xīnniáng	bride
天生	tiānshēng	be born with
敬	jìng	propose a toast to
顺利	shùnlì	smoothly
庆祝	qìngzhù	celebrate

Additional Expressions

Chinese Zodiac

鼠	shǔ	Rat
牛	niú	Ox
虎	hǔ	Tiger
兔	tù	Rabbit
龙	lóng	Dragon
蛇	shé	Snake
马	mǎ	Horse
羊	yáng	Goat
猴	hóu	Monkey
鸡	jī	Rooster
狗	gǒu	Dog
猪	zhū	Pig

Occasions on Which Chinese Invite People to Dinner

Chinese people usually invite other people to dinner on occasions such as festival celebrations, weddings, funerals, births, birthday parties and gatherings of relatives and good friends, as well as a child's entrance into a higher school, one's own promotion or farewells.

10 乘飞机 chéng fēijī
Taking a Plane

Basic Sentences

55. 请到这边来一下。
    Qǐng dào zhèbian lái yíxià.
    Please come over here.

56. 这是我的私人用品。
    Zhè shì wǒ de sīrén yòngpǐn.
    These are my personal belongings.

57. 里面有酒或香烟吗？
    Lǐmiàn yǒu jiǔ huò xiāngyān ma?
    Is there any alcohol or cigarettes in it?

58. 应该在哪里换登机牌？
    Yīnggāi zài nǎlǐ huàn dēngjīpái?
    Where should I get my boarding pass?

59. 哪里能吃饭？
    Nǎlǐ néng chī fàn?
    Where can I have something to eat?

60. 请问行李寄存处在哪里？
    Qǐngwèn xíngli jìcúnchù zài nǎlǐ?
    May I ask ... is there a cloakroom anywhere?

C: 工作人员（*Customs Officer*）
T: 乘　　客（*Traveler*）

Dialogues

(1) 工作人员检查旅行箱 (gōngzuò rényuán jiǎnchá lǚxíngxiāng)

T: 先生，请到这边来一下。请打开您的箱子。这些是什么？
(Xiānsheng, qǐng dào zhèbian lái yíxià. Qǐng dǎkāi nín de xiāngzi. Zhèxiē shì shénme?)

C: 这是我的私人用品。那些是送给朋友的礼品。
(Zhè shì wǒ de sīrén yòngpǐn. Nàxiē shì sòng gěi péngyou de lǐpǐn.)

T: 里面有酒或香烟吗？
(Lǐmiàn yǒu jiǔ huò xiāngyān ma?)

C: 有一瓶酒和一条香烟。
(Yǒu yì píng jiǔ hé yì tiáo xiāngyān.)

T: 好的，您可以走了。
(Hǎo de, nín kěyǐ zǒu le.)

(2) 转机 (zhuǎnjī)

T: 我刚坐CA 984次航班到北京，要换乘今天下午3点半飞广州的CZ 3104次航班，应该在哪里换登机牌？
(Wǒ gāng zuò CA jiǔ bā sì cì hángbān dào Běijīng, yào huànchéng jīntiān xiàwǔ sān diǎn bàn fēi Guǎnzhōu de CZ sān yāo líng sì cì hángbān, yīnggāi zài nǎlǐ huàn dēngjīpái?)

(1) Checking Suitcases

C: Please come over here, sir. Please open your suitcase. What are these?

T: These are my personal belongings. Those are gifts for my friends.

C: Is there any alcohol or cigarettes in it?

T: One bottle of wine and a carton of cigarettes.

C: OK, you can go now.

(2) Changing Flights

T: I've just arrived in Beijing by CA 984. I'll be flying to Guangzhou by CZ 3104 at three thirty this afternoon. Where should I get my boarding pass?

C: Qǐng nín zài xiàwǔ liǎng diǎn qián dào H hào guìtái
请您在下午两点前到H号柜台
huàn dēngjīpái.
换登机牌。

T: Xièxie. Qǐngwèn H hào guìtái zài nǎr?
谢谢。请问H号柜台在哪儿?

C: Wǎng qián zǒu, zài zuǒbian.
往前走,在左边。

T: Nǎlǐ néng chī fàn?
哪里能吃饭?

C: Zhèbian xiàqù dōu shì cāntīng. Nǐ kěyǐ
这边下去都是餐厅。你可以
zìjǐ xuǎn.
自己选。

T: Qǐngwèn xíngli jìcúnchù zài nǎlǐ?
请问行李寄存处在哪里?

C: Zài èr céng dàtīng gōnggòng qūyù de dōngbian.
在二层大厅公共区域的东边。

C: You can get your boarding pass at the Counter H before two o'clock this afternoon.

T: Thank you. Where is Counter H?

C: Go straight ahead. On the left side.

T: Where can I have something to eat?

C: There are restaurants down from there. You may choose one.

T: May I ask ... is there a cloakroom anywhere?

C: To the east of the public area of the hall on the second floor.

New Words

礼品	lǐpǐn	gift
香烟	xiāngyān	cigarette
航班	hángbān	flight
换乘	huànchéng	trasfer to (a bus, train, etc)
登机牌	dēngjīpái	boarding pass
柜台	guìtái	counter
寄存处	jìcúnchù	cloakroom

Additional Expressions

Flying Abroad

出境	chūjìng	leave a country
现金	xiànjīn	cash
关税	guānshuì	customs duty
免税品	miǎnshuìpǐn	duty-free goods
上税	shàngshuì	pay taxes
珠宝	zhūbǎo	jewellery
申报	shēnbào	declare
申报单	shēnbàodān	declaration form
航班号	hángbānhào	flight number

TIP

Major Airlines

Name	English Abbreviation	Chinese Abbreviation
Air China (China)	CA	国航
China Southern Airlines (China)	CZ	南航
China Eastern Airlines (China)	MU	东航
China Airlines (Taiwan, China)	CI	中华航空
Cathay Pacific Airways (HongKong, China)	CX	国泰航空
American Airlines (USA)	AA	美航
Air France (France)	AF	法航
British Airways (UK)	BA	英航
Lufthansa German Airlines (Germany)	LH	汉莎航空
Japan Airlines (Japan)	JL	日航
Korean Airlines (The Republic of Korea)	KE	大韩航空

NOTE

11 chéng huǒchē 乘火车
Taking a Train

Basic Sentences

61. Wǒ zhǎo bu zháo qù Shànghǎi de hòuchēshì.
    我找不着去上海的候车室。
    I can't find the waiting room for passengers going to Shanghai.

62. Chēcì shì duōshao?
    车次是多少？
    What's your train number?

63. Tíqián bàn xiǎoshí kāishǐ jiǎnpiào.
    提前半小时开始检票。
    The check-in starts half an hour before departure.

64. Nín qù Shànghǎi chūchāi ma?
    您去上海出差吗？
    Are you going to Shanghai on business?

65. Qù de dìfang bǐ wǒ hái duō ne!
    去的地方比我还多呢！
    You've been to more places than I have.

66. Wǒ jīnnián dōngtiān yídìng qù yí tàng.
    我今年冬天一定去一趟。
    I'll go there this winter, too.

M: 马 克 (Mark)   A: 工作人员 (Attendant)
T: 旅 客 (Traveler)

Dialogues

xúnzhǎo hòuchēshì
(1) 寻找候车室

M: Nín hǎo! Dà píngmù shang de zì tài kuài le,
您好！大屏幕上的字太快了，
wǒ zhǎo bu zháo qù Shànghǎi de hòuchēshì.
我找不着去上海的候车室。

A: Chēcì shì duōshao?
车次是多少？

M: G yī cì.
G1次。

A: G yī cì zài èr lóu de dì-èr hòuchēshì.
G1次在二楼的第二候车室。
Tíqián bàn xiǎoshí kāishǐ jiǎnpiào.
提前半小时开始检票。

M: Míngbai le, xièxie!
明白了，谢谢！

zài huǒchē shang hé biérén liáotiānr
(2) 在火车上和别人聊天儿

M: Nín qù Shànghǎi chūchāi ma?
您去上海出差吗？

T: Ò, wǒ lái Běijīng chūchāi, xiànzài huí
哦，我来北京出差，现在回
Shànghǎi. Nǐ shì xuésheng ma?
上海。你是学生吗？

M: Ò, wǒ zǎo jiù gōngzuò le.
哦，我早就工作了。

(1) Looking for the Waiting Room

M: Hello. The words on the screen are moving too fast. I can't find the waiting room for passengers going to Shanghai.

A: What's your train number?

M: G 1.

A: The waiting room for G 1 is Waiting Room Two on the second floor. Please note that the check-in starts half an hour before departure.

M: I see. Thank you.

(2) Chatting on the Train

M: Are you going to Shanghai on business?

T: Well, I came to Beijing on business, and I'm now going back to Shanghai. Are you a student?

M: No, I started working a long time ago.

T: 你不是第一次来中国吧?

M: 不是。

T: 你都去过哪些地方?

M: 天津、西安、洛阳、哈尔滨、青岛,还有云南和海南。

T: 嗬,去的地方比我还多呢!哈尔滨怎么样?

M: 我是冬天去的,很冷,可是冰灯很漂亮。

T: 是吗?我今年冬天一定要去一趟。

T: It's not your first time in China, is it?

M: No.

T: What places have you been to?

M: Tianjin, Xi'an, Luoyang, Harbin, Qingdao and Yunnan, as well as Hainan.

T: Oh, you've been to more places than I have. How is Harbin?

M: I went there in winter and it was very cold, but the ice sculptures were really beautiful.

T: Really? I'll go there this winter, too.

New Words

屏幕	píngmù	screen
候车室	hòuchēshì	waiting room
车次	chēcì	train number
提前	tíqián	in advance
检票	jiǎnpiào	check in
出差	chūchāi	travel on business

Additional Expressions

Phrases About Train

特快列车	tèkuài lièchē	express train
动车(高速铁路)	dòngchē (gāosù tiělù)	China Railway High-speed
软卧	ruǎnwò	soft sleeper
硬卧	yìngwò	hard sleeper
硬座	yìngzuò	hard seat
餐车	cānchē	dining car
站台	zhàntái	railway platform

Train Types and Speed in China

Gaosu Tielu are known as China Railway Highspeed trains (Abbreviated as CRH), and their speed is mostly 200 to 350 kilometers per hour. The speed of these new type trains has already exceeded 500 kilometers per hour. In line with the actual need for train speed, train types can be further divided into G-High-Speed Multiple Unit, D-Multiple Unit and C-Intercity Trains.

Express trains in China are divided into Direct Express (Z-Direct Express) and Ordinary Express (T-Air-Conditioned Express). The maximum speed of Direct Express trains may reach 160 kilometers per hour, and they may not stop at any station. The speed of T-Air-Conditioned Express trains may also reach 160 kilometers per hour, but they stop at some major stations.

The maximum speed of the fast trains (K-Air-Conditioned Fast Trains) is 120 kilometers per hour. Ordinary passenger train are also called ordinary fast trains and are distinguished by the lack of a Latin alphabet letter before the train numbers. They run the slowest at 120 kilometers an hour. They stop at more stations than fast trains, and the slowest trains stop at every station they pass.

Trains whose train numbers start with Y and N are very rare, and they usually travel only within a province. A real-name system has been adopted in China for those buying train tickets, and valid personal IDs have to be provided at the time of pruchase.

12 乘坐市内交通工具
chéngzuò shì nèi jiāotōng gōngjù

Taking Public Transportation in the City

Basic Sentences

67. 这辆车去不去天安门？
Zhè liàng chē qù bu qù Tiān'ānmén?
Does this bus go to Tian'anmen?

68. 您刷卡还是买票？
Nín shuākǎ háishi mǎi piào?
Will you use your card or buy a ticket?

69. 到站时能叫我一下吗？
Dào zhàn shí néng jiào wǒ yíxià ma?
Would you please tell me if I get there?

70. 下车的乘客请做好准备。
Xià chē de chéngkè qǐng zuòhǎo zhǔnbèi.
Passengers for this stop, please get ready to leave.

71. 您好，您去哪儿？
Nín hǎo, nín qù nǎr?
Hello. Where are you going?

72. 这是您的发票，请收好。
Zhè shì nín de fāpiào, qǐng shōuhǎo.
Here's your receipt. Please keep it.

M: 马 克 (*Mark*)   C: 售票员 (*Conductor*)
D: 司 机 (*Driver*)

Dialogues

(1) 在公共汽车上
zài gōnggòng qìchē shang

M: 请问，这辆车去不去天安门？
Qǐngwèn, zhè liàng chē qù bu qù Tiān'ānmén?

C: 这车不去天安门。您可以在动物园换12路。您刷卡还是买票？
Zhè chē bú qù Tiān'ānmén. Nín kěyǐ zài dòngwùyuán huàn shí'èr lù. Nín shuākǎ háishi mǎi piào?

M: 我忘了带卡，我买张到动物园的票吧。
Wǒ wàngle dài kǎ, wǒ mǎi zhāng dào dòngwùyuán de piào ba.

C: 两块。这是5块，找您3块，请拿好。
Liǎng kuài. Zhè shì wǔ kuài, zhǎo nín sān kuài, qǐng náhǎo.

M: 请问我要坐几站？
Qǐngwèn wǒ yào zuò jǐ zhàn?

C: 坐6站。
Zuò liù zhàn.

M: 谢谢。到站时能叫我一下吗？
Xièxie. Dào zhàn shí néng jiào wǒ yíxià ma?

C: 没问题。我们也有电子报站。
Méi wèntí. Wǒmen yě yǒu diànzǐ bàozhàn.

(1) On a Bus

M: Excuse me, does this bus go to Tian'anmen?

C: This bus doesn't go to Tian'anmen. You can transfer to Bus No. 12 at the zoo. Will you use your card or buy a ticket?

M: I forget to take my card with me. One ticket to the zoo, please.

C: Two yuan. This is five yuan. Here's your change, three yuan.

M: Please tell me how many stops before I get there.

C: Six stops.

M: Would you please tell me if I get there?

C: No problem. We also have an electronic system for announcing the stops.

(dào dòngwùyuán zhàn)
(到 动物园 站)

(Diànzǐ bàozhàn shēng:"Dòngwùyuán dào le, xià chē
(电子报站 声:"动物园 到了,下车
de chéngkè qǐng zuòhǎo zhǔnbèi.")
的乘客请做好准备。")

(duì Mǎkè) Nà wèi xiānsheng, dòngwùyuán
C:(对马克)那位先生,动物园
zhàn dào le, gāi xià chē le!
站到了,该下车了!

zuò chūzūchē
(2) 坐 出 租 车

Nín hǎo, nín qù nǎr?
D:您好,您去哪儿?

Wǒ qù Xú Bēihóng jìniànguǎn.
M:我去徐悲鸿纪念馆。

(zài chē shang)
(在车上)

Qǐngwèn yíxià, qù Xú Bēihóng jìniànguǎn
M:请问一下,去徐悲鸿纪念馆
dàgài duōshao qián?
大概多少钱?

Dàigài liùshí duō. Nín cóng nǎr lái?
D:大概60多。您从哪儿来?

Cóng Bālí lái.
M:从巴黎来。

(arriving at the zoo)

(Recording: "We have arrived at the zoo. Passengers for this stop, please get ready to leave.")

C: *(to Mark)* Sir, we've arrived at the zoo. You can get off the bus here.

(2) Taking a Taxi

D: Hello. Where are you going?

M: I'm going to the Xu Beihong Memorial Hall.

(in the car)

M: Excuse me, but about how much is it to the Xu Beihong Memorial Hall?

D: About sixty yuan. Where are you from?

M: Paris.

D: 来北京玩儿？

M: 也算是吧。我来工作，也喜欢旅游。

D: 您都去过哪儿？

M: 南边北边我去过不少地方了，下一步打算去新疆和西藏看看。

D: 昨天我送一对外国夫妇去机场，他们就是去西藏玩儿的。

（到达徐悲鸿纪念馆）

D: 一共61块钱。（接钱）钱正好，这是您的发票，请收好。再见！

M: 再见！

D: Did you come to Beijing for a vacation?

M: In a way, yes. I've come to work, but I also like travelling.

D: What places have you been to?

M: I've been to many places in the North and the South. I plan to go to Xinjiang and Tibet next to have a look.

D: I sent a foreign couple to the airport yesterday. They were travelling to Tibet.

(arriving at the Xu Beihong Memorial Hall)

D: Sixty one yuan in all. *(taking the money)* Exactly right. Here's your receipt. Please keep it. Goodbye.

M: Bye-bye.

New Words

刷卡	shuākǎ	swipe card
纪念馆	jìniànguǎn	memorial hall
夫妇	fūfù	husband and wife
正好	zhènghǎo	just right; exactly
发票	fāpiào	receipt

Additional Expressions

Traveling

车站	chēzhàn	station; stop
站牌	zhànpái	station sign
打车	dǎchē	take a taxi
步行	bùxíng	walk
地铁	dìtiě	subway
搭车	dāchē	get a ride; hitchhike
背包客	bēibāokè	backpacker

Subways in China

China's first subway line started its trial operation in Beijing in October of 1969. The Tianjin subway started its formal operations in February of 1976. Shanghai Metro Line 1 opened to traffic in April of 1995. Guangzhou Metro line 1 opened to traffic on June 28th, 1999. Right now in cities such as Nanjing, Shenyang, Chengdu, Wuhan, Xi'an, Chongqing, Shenzhen and Suzhou, subway lines have already been opened. In many other cities, subways are either under construction or in the planning stage. The Hong Kong subway opened to traffic in 1979. The Taipei subway started construction in 1988 and started trial operations in 1995.

China's subways have developed very rapidly and are highly appreciated by the public because they have solved the public transportation problem. A unified price system has been adopted by the Beijing subway in an attempt to encourage people to use public transportation means. Riders need pay only one small fee to go anywhere on any line, as long as they change lines underground without leaving the station.

NOTE

13 在酒店
At the Hotel

Basic Sentences

73. 您预订过吗?
Nín yùdìngguo ma?
Have you made a reservation?

74. 请填写住宿卡。
Qǐng tiánxiě zhùsùkǎ.
Please fill in this form.

75. 我想要一个双人间。
Wǒ xiǎng yào yí gè shuāngrénjiān.
I'd like to have a double room.

76. 房费都含早餐。
Fángfèi dōu hán zǎocān.
Breakfast is included in all room rates.

77. 下午两点以前办理退房手续。
Xiàwǔ liǎng diǎn yǐqián bànlǐ tuì fáng shǒuxù.
Please check out before two o'clock.

78. 发票的名称怎么写?
Fāpiào de míngchēng zěnme xiě?
What name should I put on the receipt?

F: 前台 (*Front Desk*) M: 马克 (*Mark*)

Dialogues

(1) 到预订的酒店入住 dào yùdìng de jiǔdiàn rùzhù

F: 您好，您预订过吗？
Nín hǎo, nín yùdìngguo ma?

M: 是的。这是我的护照。
Shì de. Zhè shì wǒ de hùzhào.

F: 有，查到了。请填写住宿卡。单人间一天350元。您住两天对吧？
Yǒu, chádào le. Qǐng tiánxiě zhùsùkǎ. Dānrénjiān yì tiān sānbǎi wǔshí yuán. Nín zhù liǎng tiān duì ba?

M: 是的，没错。
Shì de, méi cuò.

F: 这是您的房卡。
Zhè shì nín de fángkǎ.

(2) 到未预订的酒店入住 dào wèi yùdìng de jiǔdiàn rùzhù

M: 您好。我想要一个双人间。
Nín hǎo. Wǒ xiǎng yào yí gè shuāngrénjiān.

F: 您要豪华间还是标准间？
Nín yào háohuájiān háishi biāozhǔnjiān?

M: 都是什么价格？
Dōu shì shénme jiàgé?

(1) Checking into a Hotel with a Reservation

F: Hello. Have you made a reservation?

M: Yes, I have. This is my passport.

F: I've found it. Please fill in this form. It's 350 yuan per day for a single room. You've reserved for two days, haven't you?

M: Yes, that's correct.

F: Here is your room card.

(2) Checking into a Hotel Without a Reservation

M: Hello. I'd like to have a double room.

F: Would you like a deluxe or standard one?

M: What are the rates?

F: 您看看这个单子，上面都有标价。房费都含早餐，标准间有网络，没有电脑；豪华间有电脑。

M: 那就豪华间吧。

F: 您住几天？

M: 三个晚上。我24号上午离开。

F: 麻烦您出示一下护照。

M: 好，这是我的护照。

F: 您需要交1500元押金，可以刷卡。

（办完押金手续后）

F: 您的入住手续已经办好了。这是房卡。

F: Look at the brochure. There are prices in it. Breakfast is included in all room rates. There is access to the Internet in the standard room, but there is no computer. The deluxe room is equipped with a computer.

M: Then I'll take the deluxe one.

F: How long do you intend to stay?

M: Three nights. I'm leaving on the 24th in the morning.

F: Would you please show me your passport?

M: Sure. Here it is.

F: You should pay a deposit of 1,500 yuan. You can use your card.

(after paying the deposit)

F: You are now finished checking in. Here is your room card.

M: 几点前退房?

F: 下午两点以前办理退房手续,不然会加收半天的房费。

M: 好的。顺便问一下,早餐的时间和地点?

F: 6点半到9点。在一楼的自助餐厅。

(3) 退房

M: 我退房。

F: 请把房卡给我。请稍等。

M: Before when should I check out?

F: Please check out before two o'clock or another half day will be charged.

M: Very good. By the way, when and where is breakfast?

F: From half past six to nine in the morning at the restaurant buffet.

(3) Checking out

M: I'm checking out.

F: May I have the room card please? Please wait a minute.

(yǔ lóucéng fúwùyuán quèrèn hòu)
(与楼层服务员确认后)

F: 先生，您使用了房间的收费商品，一瓶啤酒和一盒方便面，再加上3天的房费，一共是1204元。您交了1500元押金，退您296元。这是您的账单，请在右下角签名。

M: 好。

F: 发票的名称怎么写？

M: 请按照我这张名片上的公司写。只写住宿费，啤酒和方便面我另外付。再帮我叫一辆去机场的出租车吧，谢谢你！

(calling the attendant of that floor)

F: Sir, you had one beer and one package of instant noodles from the room's extra provisions. Added to the three day room rate the total is 1,204 yuan. You gave a 1,500 yuan deposit, so we will refund you 296 yuan. Here is the bill. Please sign at the bottom right corner.

M: OK.

F: What name should I put on the receipt?

M: It'll be fine if you put the name of the company that's on my card. Please just put the room rate, I'll pay for the beer and instant noodles separately. Would you please call a taxi for me to go to the airport? Thank you!

New Words

预订	yùdìng	reserve
豪华间	háohuájiān	deluxe room
标准间	biāozhǔnjiān	standard room
标价	biāojià	marked price
押金	yājīn	deposit
手续	shǒuxù	procedure
签名	qiānmíng	signature

Additional Expressions

The Common Parts of a Hotel

前台	qiántái	reception
大堂	dàtáng	lobby
套房	tàofáng	suite
咖啡厅	kāfēitīng	coffee house
大床房	dàchuángfáng	double-bed room
康乐中心	kānglè zhōngxīn	health club
商务中心	shāngwù zhōngxīn	business center
无线上网	wúxiàn shàngwǎng	wireless Internet access

Some Five-star Hotels in Beijing

Fèi'ěrméng Jiǔdiàn
费尔蒙酒店
Fairmont Hotel
8 Yong'an Dongli, Jianguomenwai Dajie, Chaoyang Qu
010-85117777

Pángǔ Qīxīng Jiǔdiàn
盘古七星酒店
Pangu Seven Star Hotel
27 Central North 4th Ring Road, Chaoyang Qu
010-84577822

Yíhé Ānmàn Jiǔdiàn
颐和安缦酒店
Aman at Summer Palace
1 Gongmen Qianjie, Haidian Qu
010-59879999

Lìjùn Jiǔdiàn
励骏酒店
Legendale Hotel
90-92 Jinbaojie, Dongcheng Qu
010-851133888

Wángfǔ Bàndǎo Jiǔdiàn
王府半岛酒店
The Peninsula Beijing
8 Goldfish Lane, Wangfujing, Dongcheng Qu
010-65128899

Lìsīkǎ'ěrdùn Jiǔdiàn
丽思卡尔顿酒店
The Ritz-Carlton Hotel
1 Jinchengfang Dongjie, Jinrongjie, Xicheng Qu
010-66016666

NOTE

cānyǐn
14 餐饮
Restaurants

Basic Sentences

Huānyíng guānglín, qǐngwèn nín jǐ wèi?
79. 欢迎光临，请问您几位？
Welcome. How many people, please?

Wǒmen xiǎng yào kào chuānghu de zuòwèi.
80. 我们想要靠窗户的座位。
We'd like to have a table by the window.

Nǐ néng tuījiàn yíxià zhèlǐ de tèsècài ma?
81. 你能推荐一下这里的特色菜吗？
Can you recommend some special dishes?

Fúwùyuán, jiézhàng!
82. 服务员，结账！
Waiter, check, please.

Nín hē diǎnr shénme?
83. 您喝点儿什么？
What would you like to drink?

Lái yì bēi wēishìjì!
84. 来一杯威士忌！
One glass of whiskey please!

A: 服务员（*Attendant*）   M: 马 克（*Mark*）

Dialogues

(1) 在饭馆 zài fànguǎn

(Mǎkè hé nǚpéngyou dào fànguǎn chī fàn.)
(马克和女朋友到饭馆吃饭。)

A: 欢迎光临，请问您几位？
Huānyíng guānglín, qǐngwèn nín jǐ wèi?

M: 两位。我们想要靠窗户的座位。
Liǎng wèi. Wǒmen xiǎng yào kào chuānghu de zuòwèi.

A: 好的，这边请。这是菜单。
Hǎo de, zhèbian qǐng. Zhè shì càidān.

M: 你能推荐一下这里的特色菜吗？
Nǐ néng tuījiàn yíxià zhèlǐ de tèsècài ma?

A: 樟茶鸭、排骨炖玉米都很好。
Zhāngcháyā、páigǔ dùn yùmǐ dōu hěn hǎo.

M: 听起来不错啊。青菜有什么？
Tīng qǐlái búcuò a. Qīngcài yǒu shénme?

A:（指菜单）在这儿。娃娃菜、油麦菜、空心菜都有。
(zhǐ càidān) Zài zhèr. Wáwacài、yóumàicài、kōngxīncài dōu yǒu.

M: 来个清炒油麦菜。
Lái gè qīngchǎo yóumàicài.

A: 您喝点儿什么？
Nín hē diǎnr shénme?

(1) At a Restaurant

(Mark and his girlfriend go to a restaurant.)

A: Welcome. How many people, please?

M: Two. We'd like to have a table by the window.

A: OK. This way, please. Here is the menu.

M: Can you recommend some special dishes?

A: *Zhangcha* duck and stewed spare ribs with corn are very good.

M: It sounds good. Do you have any green vegetables?

A: *(pointing at the menu)* Here you are. We have *wawacai*, *youmaicai* and *kongxincai* *(three kinds of green vegetables)*.

M: One stir-fried *youmaicai*.

A: What would you like to drink?

M: Yào yì bēi xiān zhà xīguāzhī ba.
要一杯鲜榨西瓜汁吧。

A: Hǎo de, qǐng shāo děng.
好的,请稍等。

(yòngcān jiéshù)
(用餐结束)

M: Fúwùyuán, jiézhàng!
服务员,结账!

A: Zhè shì zhàngdān, yígòng yìbǎi yīshísì yuán.
这是账单,一共 114 元。

(2) 在酒吧 zài jiǔbā

A: Nín hǎo, nín hē diǎnr shénme?
您好,您喝点儿什么?

M: Lái yì bēi wēishìjì!
来一杯威士忌!

A: Jiā bīng ma?
加冰吗?

M: Jiā. Jīntiān yǒu huódòng ma?
加。今天有活动吗?

A: Yǒu, 10 diǎn yǒu yí gè tiáojiǔ biǎoyǎn.
有,10点有一个调酒表演。

M: Zhèlǐ shì bu shì yèlǐ yī diǎn guānmén?
这里是不是夜里1点关门?

A: Xiànzài yáncháng dào yèlǐ liǎng diǎn le.
现在延长到夜里两点了。

M: A mug of fresh watermelon juice.

A: OK, just one moment.

(after the meal)

M: Waiter, check, please.

A: Here is the check. 114 yuan in total.

(2) In a Bar

A: Hello. What would you like to drink?

M: One glass of whiskey, please.

A: On the rocks?

M: Yes. Are there any planned activities today?

A: Yes, there is a show of fancy bartending at ten o'clock.

M: This place closes at one o'clock, right?

A: It's now been extended to two o'clock in the morning.

New Words

靠	kào	near; close to
推荐	tuījiàn	recommend
特色菜	tèsècài	special type of food in a restaurant
鲜榨	xiān zhà	freshly squeezed (juice)
稍等	shāo děng	Wait a minute.
结账	jiézhàng	pay the check
调酒	tiáojiǔ	mixology
延长	yáncháng	prolong

Additional Expressions

Cooking Ingredients

油	yóu	oil
盐	yán	salt
糖	táng	sugar
醋	cù	vinegar
酱油	jiàngyóu	soy sauce
辣椒	làjiāo	chili sauce
味精	wèijīng	MSG
胡椒粉	hújiāofěn	pepper
番茄酱	fānqiéjiàng	ketchup

 **Some Famous Restaurants in Beijing**

Quánjùdé Kǎoyādiàn
全聚德烤鸭店
Quanjude Roast Duck Restaurant
- ✧ Beijing roast duck
- ✉ 30 Qianmen Dajie, Dongcheng Qu
- ☎ 010-65112418

Kǒng Yǐjǐ Jiǔdiàn
孔乙己酒店
Kong Yiji Restaurant
- ✧ Shaoxing-style cooking
- ✉ 2A Dongming Hutong, Denei Dajie, Xicheng Qu
- ☎ 010-66184917

Xīnjiāng Fàndiàn
新疆饭店
Xinjiang Restaurant
- ✧ Xinjiang-style cooking
- ✉ 7 Sanlihe Lu, Xicheng Qu
- ☎ 010-68335599

Shànghǎi Lǎo Fàndiàn
上海老饭店
Shanghai Classical Hotel
- ✧ Shanghai-style cooking
- ✉ 5 Sanlihe Donglu, Xicheng Qu
- ☎ 010-68587777

Fèiténgyúxiāng
沸腾鱼乡
Feitengyuxiang Restaurant
- ✧ Sichuan-style cooking
- ✉ 17 Zhichun Lu, Haidian Qu
- ☎ 010-82311286

* There is no service charge in ordinary hotels and restaurants in China except for a few big ones. There is also no tipping in restaurants in China.

NOTE

15 打电话 dǎ diànhuà
Making Telephone Calls

Basic Sentences

85. Duì, shì wǒ. Nǐ shì Mǎkè ba?
对，是我。你是马克吧？
Yes, it's me. You're Mark, right?

86. Wèi, nín hǎo, nín zhǎo nǎ wèi?
喂，您好，您找哪位？
Hello. Who do you want to speak to?

87. Qǐngwèn Wáng Ān'ān zài ma?
请问王安安在吗？
Is Wang An'an in?

88. Qǐngwèn nín shì nǎ wèi?
请问您是哪位？
Who's calling, please?

89. Nín yǒu shìr ma? Wǒ kěyǐ zhuǎngào tā.
您有事儿吗？我可以转告她。
Do you have a message that I can pass on to her?

90. Nín dǎcuò le.
您打错了。
You dialed the wrong number.

M: 马 克（Mark） W: 王安安（Wang An'an）
WM: 王安安的母亲（Wang's Mother）
B: 白 梅（Bai Mei） R: 接电话人（Receiver）

Dialogues

(1) 熟人接电话 shúrén jiē diànhuà

（马克打手机。Mǎkè dǎ shǒujī.）

M: 喂，是王安安吗？
Wèi, shì Wáng Ān'ān ma?

W: 对，是我。你是马克吧？好久没联系了。
Duì, shì wǒ. Nǐ shì Mǎkè ba? Hǎojiǔ méi liánxì le.

M: 这个周末有空儿吗？咱们约几个人一起爬长城吧，金山岭长城！
Zhège zhōumò yǒu kòngr ma? Zánmen yuē jǐ gè rén yìqǐ pá Chángchéng ba, Jīnshānlǐng Chángchéng!

W: 好啊。
Hǎo a.

(2) 转告信息 zhuǎngào xìnxī

（王安安的母亲在家接电话。Wáng Ān'ān de mǔqīn zài jiā jiē diànhuà.）

WM: 喂，您好，您找哪位？
Wèi, nín hǎo, nín zhǎo nǎ wèi?

M: 您好。请问王安安在吗？
Nín hǎo. Qǐngwèn Wáng Ān'ān zài ma?

(1) Calling an Old Acquaintance

(Mark is making a call on his cell phone.)

M: Hello. Is that Wang An'an?

W: Yes, it's me. You're Mark, right? It's been a long time since we were last in touch.

M: Are you free this weekend? Let's go and climb the Great Wall together with a few others – the Great Wall at Jinshanling.

W: Good idea.

(2) Leaving a Message

(Wang An'an's mother is answering a call at home.)

WM: Hello. Who do you want to speak to?

M: Hello. Is Wang An'an in?

WM: 抱歉,她出去了。请问您是哪位?

M: 我是她的朋友马克。她手机没人接,短信也没回,所以我打到家里来了。

WM: 她真是个马大哈,今天忘了带手机。您有事儿吗?我可以转告她。

M: 明天下午两点钟的聚会,希望她准时参加。

WM: 好的,我一定转告。谢谢您!

M: 不用谢,再见!

WM: Sorry, she is out. Who's calling, please?

M: I'm her friend Mark. There is no answer on her cell phone, and she didn't respond to my short message, so I called here.

WM: She's so careless. She forgot to take the cell phone with her. Do you have a message that I can pass on to her?

M: It's about the get-together at two o'clock tomorrow afternoon. We hope she can make it.

WM: OK. I'll let her know. Thank you!

M: You are welcome. Bye!

(3) 打错电话

（白梅给某公司打电话。）

B: 喂！请问王明在吗？

R: 王明？这儿没有叫王明的。

B: 这儿不是四达公司吗？

R: 不是，您打错了。

B: 对不起！

(3) Dialing the Wrong Number

(Bai Mei is trying to make a call to a company.)

B: Hello. Is Wang Ming in?

R: Wang Ming? There is no Wang Ming here.

B: Isn't this Sida Company?

R: No. You dialed the wrong number.

B: Sorry.

New Words

联系	liánxì	contact
短信	duǎnxìn	short message serivce
马大哈	mǎdàhā	careless person
转告	zhuǎngào	pass on (message)
聚会	jùhuì	party
准时	zhǔnshí	on time

Additional Expressions

Phrases About Telephone

占线	zhànxiàn	The line is busy.
关机	guānjī	power off
开机	kāijī	power on
静音	jìngyīn	mute
没电了	méi diàn le	no power

电池	diànchí	battery
充电	chōngdiàn	charge
信号不好	xìnhào bù hǎo	signal is not good

Making International Calls with Mobile Phones in China

To make international long distance calls with a mobile phone in China, one has to subscribe to an international long distance call service first. After subscribing to the service one should:

1. Dial IP number as follows: IP number + 00 + country or district code + city code + number of the landline telephone.
2. Direct dial is as follows: 00 + country or district code + number of the landline telephone.

Charging standard:

1. As of 2012, the rate for direct dial is 0.80 yuan every 6 seconds, but preferential prices are given based on different time periods and legal holidays of different countries. For more specific deals, refer to the public announcements

of the local mobile company.

2. You can also refer to the public announcements of the local mobile company.

IP telephones are also very popular .You can buy an IP card at a newsstand by the roadside or in a supermarket and use it to make calls following the directions on the card. IP telephones are cheaper than using a mobile phone. Making calls by g-mail online is both cheap and convenient, but of course, using chat tools such as Skype and MSN are free of charge.

NOTE

16 gòuwù
购 物
Shopping

> **Basic Sentences**

Nín chuān duō dà hào de?
91. 您穿多大号的？
What's your size?

Jiàgé néng yōuhuì ma?
92. 价格能优惠吗？
Can I get a better price?

Gěi nín xiàopiào, shōuyíntái zài nàbian.
93. 给您小票，收银台在那边。
Here you are. The Cashier Counter is over there.

Píngguǒ zěnme mài?
94. 苹果怎么卖？
How much are these apples?

Hái yào diǎnr bié de ma?
95. 还要点儿别的吗？
What else would you like?

Shénme shíhou néng zài jìnhuò?
96. 什么时候能再进货？
When will you get more in?

M: 马 克 (*Mark*)   S: 售货员 (*Saleswoman*)
B: 白 梅 (*Bai Mei*)   V: 摊 主 (*Vendor*)

Dialogues

zài shāngdiàn mǎi yīfu
(1) 在商店买衣服

Qǐngwèn, zhè jiàn T xù duōshao qián?
M: 请问，这件T恤多少钱？

Liùbǎi'èr. Nín chuān duō dà hào de? Kěyǐ shì yíxià.
S: 620。您穿多大号的？可以试一下。

Zhōngguó de hàomǎ wǒ bù qīngchu, shì gè zuì dà hào de ba.
M: 中国的号码我不清楚，试个最大号的吧。

Dà hào de yīnggāi jiù kěyǐ. Xǐhuan shénme yánsè de?
S: 大号的应该就可以。喜欢什么颜色的？

Huángsè de.
M: 黄色的。

Nín shìshi zhè jiàn.
S: 您试试这件。

(Mǎkè shì chuān hòu)
（马克试穿后）

Duō héshì a! Chuānshang zhēn jīngshen!
S: 多**合适**啊！穿上真**精神**！

Jiàgé néng yōuhuì ma?
M: 价格能**优惠**吗？

(1) Shopping at a Franchised Store

M: Excuse me, how much does this T-shirt cost?

S: 620 yuan. What's your size? You can try one on.

M: I have no idea about size numbers in China. Let me try the biggest size.

S: I think large will do. What color do you like?

M: Yellow.

S: Try this one.

(after trying on the T-shirt)

S: What a good fit! You look great.

M: Can I get a better price?

S: 我们是专卖店，不讲价。现在的价格就是优惠价，原价680。

M: 那就要这件吧。

S:（开票）给您小票，收银台在那边。

（马克付钱以后，把交款单交给售货员。）

S: 小票请收好。一个星期内，如果有质量问题，可以凭票退换。欢迎您再来！

(2) 在水果摊上买水果

B: 师傅，苹果怎么卖？

V: 4块钱1斤。瞧这些苹果多好，又大又红，又甜又脆。

S: There is no bargain since this is a franchised store. This present price is already discounted. It sold originally for 680 yuan.

M: I'll take this then.

S: *(writing the bill)* Here you are. The Cashier Counter is over there.

(After paying the bill, Mark gives the receipt to the saleswoman.)

S: Keep the receipt. If there is any quality problem, you can return or exchange it within one week by showing this receipt. Please come back again.

(2) Buying Fruit from a Vendor

B: Hello. How much are these apples?

V: 4 yuan a *jin (1 jin is equal to 500g)*. Look, how nice these apples are! They are big and red, sweet and crisp.

B: 是不错。(选了几个)就这些吧。

V: 一共3斤6两,再来1个,凑4斤吧。

B: 好,加上这个。

V: 4斤1两,算4斤。一共16块钱。还要点儿别的吗?

B: 不要了。给您钱。

V: 20块,找您4块。

(3) 在书店,马克想买DVD

M: 您好,这儿有中国民乐的DVD吗?

S: 有很多啊。这种卖得最好。有精装的,也有简装的。

B: Really nice. *(Having chosen a few)* Just these.

V: Altogether 3.6 *jin*. Let me add another apple and make it 4 *jin*.

B: OK. Add this one.

V: 4.1 *jin*, but let's just say 4 *jin*. Altogether 16 yuan. What else would you like?

B: Nothing else. Here's the money.

V: 20 yuan. Here's your change, 4 yuan.

(3) Mark Wants to Buy DVD at a Bookstore

M: Hello. Do you have a Chinese folk music DVD?

S: We have a lot. This one is the best seller. We have both the casebound and plain packet.

M: 我要简装的。您这儿还有《中国简史》吗?

S: 对不起,刚刚卖完。

M: 什么时候能再进货?

S: 大概得一个星期。您真不简单,还看中文书啊?

M: 我哪有那个水平!我是帮朋友买的。

M: I'd like the plain packet one. Do you also have *A Brief History of China*?

S: Sorry, that was just sold out.

M: When will you get more in?

S: In about a week. You are really marvelous. Do you also read Chinese books?

M: I haven't got to that point yet. I'm buying for my friend.

New Words

合适	héshì	(clothes) fit
精神	jīngshen	vigorous
优惠	yōuhuì	discount
专卖店	zhuānmàidiàn	franchised store
讲价	jiǎngjià	bargain
质量	zhìliàng	quality
退换	tuìhuàn	exchange a purchase
精装	jīngzhuāng	hardcover
简装	jiǎnzhuāng	paperback

Additional Expressions

Fabric

皮	pí	leather
棉	mián	cotton
麻	má	flax
化纤	huàxiān	chemical fiber
羊毛	yángmáo	wool
羊绒	yángróng	cashmere
真丝	zhēnsī	silk
羽绒	yǔróng	down

Classification of Shopping Centers in China

If you go shopping in China you may find the price of goods varies greatly between shopping malls and shopping on the streets.

In shopping malls you not only can get goods of fine quality, but you can also enjoy good service and a better shopping environment. If you find any quality problems with the things you purchase, you can go back to exchange or simply return them. Naturally, the prices in those malls are relatively high, though at present many shopping malls have begun giving discounts and other promotions. Some well-known shopping malls in Beijing are the Oriental Plaza and New Dong'an Market in the Wangfujing Commercial Area, Zhongyou Department Store and Juntai Department Store in the Xidan Commercial Area, and Youyi Shopping City and Pacific Department Store in the Beijing-Lufthansa Commercial Area.

What attracts people most about shopping on the streets are the low prices and the chance to bargain. But there is no guaranteeing the quality of what is bought. Those places are also usually very noisy and services varies from place to place. The following are well-known shopping streets in Beijing: Silk Market and Lady's Street.

17 guàng jiē 逛街
Strolling Around

Basic Sentences

Nín zhèr yǒu Yīngwén de guānguāng zhǐnán ma?
97. 您这儿有英文的观光指南吗?
Do you have a tourist guidebook in English?

Fùjìn yǒu zhídé yí kàn de dìfang ma?
98. 附近有值得一看的地方吗?
Is there any place worth visiting near here?

Nín néng bāng wǒ pāi zhāng zhàopiānr ma?
99. 您能帮我拍张照片儿吗?
Could you take a photo for me, please?

Bǎ zhè zuò tǎ zhào jìnlái, wǒ zhàn qiánmiàn.
100. 把这座塔照进来,我站前面。
Make this pagoda in the photo. I'll stand here, in front of it.

Zhǔnbèi hǎo le ma? Yī, èr, sān.
101. 准备好了吗?一、二、三。
Are you ready? One, two, three.

Dàizǒu háishi zài zhèr chī?
102. 带走还是在这儿吃?
Will you take it away or eat it here?

B: 白 梅 (Bai Mei)   S: 师 傅 (Seller)
P: 路 人 (Passerby)   M: 马 克 (Mark)
O: 老 板 (Owner)

Dialogues

zài jiē shang de bàotíng
(1) 在街上的报亭

B: Shīfu, wǒ mǎi yì zhāng Běijīng dìtú. Nín zhèr yǒu Yīngwén de guānguāng zhǐnán ma?
师傅，我买一张北京地图。您这儿有英文的观光指南吗？

S: Yǒu, yígòng èrshí kuài qián.
有，一共20块钱。

B: Fùjìn yǒu zhídé yí kàn de dìfang ma?
附近有值得一看的地方吗？

S: Wǎng qián bù yuǎn jiù shì Yōnghé Gōng, fùjìn hái yǒu Dìtán Gōngyuán.
往前不远就是雍和宫，附近还有地坛公园。

B: Zhè tiáo jiē jiào shénme míngzi?
这条街叫什么名字？

S: Dōngzhíménnèi Dàjiē.
东直门内大街。

B: Nǎr kěyǐ qǐng dǎoyóu a? Huì shuō Yīngwén de.
哪儿可以请导游啊？会说英文的。

S: Yōnghé Gōng li jiù yǒu, nín dào nàr wènwen ba.
雍和宫里就有，您到那儿问问吧。

(1) At the News Stand

B: Hello. I'd like one Beijing map. Do you have a tourist guidebook in English?

S: Yes. 20 yuan altogether.

B: Is there any place worth visiting near here?

S: The Yonghegong Lama Temple is just a short distance away. There is also Ditan Park not far away.

B: What's the name of the street?

S: Dongzhimennei Street.

B: Where can I hire an English-speaking guide?

S: There are guides in the Yonghegong Lama Temple. You can go and ask.

(2) pāizhào 拍照

B: Dǎrǎo yíxià, nín néng bāng wǒ pāi zhāng zhàopiānr ma?
打扰一下,您能帮我拍张照片儿吗?

P: Méi wèntí. Zài nǎr zhào?
没问题。在哪儿照?

B: Bǎ zhè zuò tǎ zhào jìnlái, wǒ zhàn qiánmiàn. Kuàimén zài zhèr.
把这座塔照进来,我站前面。快门在这儿。

P: Hǎo, zhǔnbèi hǎo le ma? Yī, èr, sān. Nín kànkan zhào de xíng bu xíng?
好,准备好了吗?一、二、三。您看看照得行不行?

B: Tǐng hǎo de, xièxie nín!
挺好的,谢谢您!

(3) pǐncháng xiǎochī 品尝 小吃

M: Lǎobǎn, bàodǔr zěnme mài?
老板,爆肚儿怎么卖?

O: Shí kuài qián yì pán. Nín lái jǐ pán?
10块钱一盘。您来几盘?

M: Liǎng pán.
两盘。

(2) Taking Photos

B: Excuse me, could you take a photo for me please?

P: With pleasure. Where would you like me to take your picture?

B: Make this pagoda in the photo. I'll stand here, in front of it. Click here.

P: OK. Are you ready? One, two, three. Have a look and see if the photo is OK.

B: Well taken. Thank you.

(3) Tasting Snacks

M: Hello. How much is the *baodu* (*quickly boiled strips of lamb*)?

O: Ten yuan a plate. How many plates do you want?

M: Two plates.

O: Dàizǒu háishi zài zhèr chī?
带走还是在这儿吃？

M: Zài zhèr chī.
在这儿吃。

O: Hǎo. （hǎn） Bàodǔr liǎng pán!
好。（喊）爆肚儿两盘！
（duì Mǎkè） Zhuō shang yǒu tiáoliào, xián dàn zìjǐ tiáo.
（对马克）桌上有调料，咸淡自己调。

O: Will you take it away or eat it here?

M: Here.

O: OK. *(in loud voice)* Two plates of *baodu*. *(to Mark)* There are spices on the table. Add them as you like.

New Words

观光	guānguāng	sightseeing
指南	zhǐnán	guidebook
值得	zhídé	worth
导游	dǎoyóu	tour guide
打扰	dǎrǎo	disturb; bother
快门	kuàimén	shutter
调料	tiáoliào	spice

Additional Expressions

Photography

相机	xiàngjī	camera
镜头	jìngtóu	lens
闪光灯	shǎnguāngdēng	flash
合影	héyǐng	group photo
半身照	bànshēnzhào	half-length photo
全身照	quánshēnzhào	full-length photo

TIP

Chinese Traditional Food

早点	**Zǎodiǎn**	**Breakfast**
烧饼	shāobing	sesame seed flatbread
油条	yóutiáo	deep-fried twisted dough sticks
包子	bāozi	steamed stuffed bun
豆包	dòubāo	steamed bun with sweetened bean paste filling
馒头	mántou	steamed bread
豆浆	dòujiāng	soybean milk
咸菜	xiáncài	preserved vegetable
咸鸭蛋	xián yādàn	salted duck egg
酱豆腐	jiàngdòufu	braised bean curd
饭类	**Fànlèi**	**Rice**
米粉	mǐfěn	boiled vermicelli noodles
米饭	mǐfàn	steamed rice
炒饭	chǎofàn	stir-fried rice
糯米饭	nuòmǐfàn	sticky rice
盖浇饭	gàijiāofàn	rice with meat and vegetables on top

面食	Miànshí	**Wheaten Food**
馄饨	húntun	wonton
面条	miàntiáo	noodle
刀削面	dāoxiāomiàn	sliced noodle
麻辣面	málàmiàn	spicy hot noodle
炸酱面	zhájiàngmiàn	noodle with fried bean sauce

汤	Tāng	**Soup**
肉汤	ròutāng	broth
鸡蛋汤	jīdàntāng	egg soup
紫菜汤	zǐcàitāng	seaweed soup
酸辣汤	suānlàtāng	hot and sour soup

小吃	Xiǎochī	**Snacks**
肉圆	ròuyuán	meatball
麻花	máhuā	fried dough twist
春卷	chūnjuǎn	spring roll
碗糕	wǎngāo	salty rice pudding
绿豆糕	lǜdòugāo	green bean cake
萝卜糕	luóbogāo	turnip cake
糖葫芦	tánghúlu	candied gourd

NOTE

18 做客 zuòkè
Being a Guest

Basic Sentences

103. Huānyíng huānyíng, kuài qǐng jìn!
欢迎欢迎,快请进!
Welcome, welcome. Please come in.

104. Zhè shì wǒmen de yìdiǎnr xīnyì.
这是我们的一点儿心意。
This is a small gift for you.

105. Nín bié máng le, wǒmen zìjǐ lái.
您别忙了,我们自己来。
You needn't go to any trouble! We can help ourselves.

106. Lái, suíbiàn chī diǎnr ba.
来,随便吃点儿吧。
Come on, help yourself.

107. Shíjiān bù zǎo le, wǒmen gāi huíqù le.
时间不早了,我们该回去了。
It's time for us to be off.

108. Bié sòng le, qǐng liúbù!
别送了,请留步!
No need to see us off. Please stay here!

W: 王安安(Wang An'an)　M: 马 克(Mark)
J: 朱 丽(Julia)
WM: 王 母(Wang's Mother)
WF: 王 父(Wang's Father)

Dialogues

shàngmén bàifǎng
(1) 上门拜访

(Mǎkè hé nǚpéngyou dào Wáng Ān'ān jiā zuòkè.)
（马克和女朋友到王安安家做客。）

W: Mǎkè, Zhūlì, huānyíng huānyíng,
马克、朱丽，欢迎欢迎，
kuài qǐng jìn! Zhè shì wǒ fùmǔ.
快请进！这是我父母。

M&J: Bófù bómǔ hǎo!
伯父伯母好！

WM: Nǐmen hǎo! Kuài qǐng zuò.
你们好！快请坐。

M: Wǒmen dàile yì píng Fǎguó pútaojiǔ,
我们带了一瓶法国葡萄酒，
qǐng shōuxià.
请收下。

WF: Zhè kě shì hǎo jiǔ a! Búguò nǐmen
这可是好酒啊！不过你们
dài lǐwù lái, tài kèqi le! Yǐhòu
带礼物来，太客气了！以后
kě bù néng zhèyàng.
可不能这样。

M: Zhè shì wǒmen de yìdiǎnr xīnyì.
这是我们的一点儿心意。
(kànkan sìzhōu) Nín jiā zhēn dà a!
（看看四周）您家真大啊！

(1) Paying Somebody a Visit

(Mark and his girlfriend are paying a visit to Wang An'an.)

- **W:** Mark, Julia, welcome, welcome. Please come in. These are my parents.
- **M&J:** Hello, Mr. and Mrs. Wang.
- **WM:** Hello. Sit down, please.
- **M:** We've brought you a bottle of French wine, please take it.
- **WF:** It's such a good wine! You're being too kind to bring a gift. You mustn't do that again.
- **M:** This is a small gift for you. *(looking around)* Your house is so spacious.

WM: <ruby>哪里<rt>Nǎlǐ</rt></ruby>，<ruby>人<rt>rén</rt></ruby><ruby>多<rt>duō</rt></ruby><ruby>了<rt>le</rt></ruby><ruby>就<rt>jiù</rt></ruby><ruby>不行<rt>bùxíng</rt></ruby><ruby>了<rt>le</rt></ruby>。<ruby>请<rt>Qǐng</rt></ruby><ruby>喝<rt>hē</rt></ruby><ruby>茶<rt>chá</rt></ruby>。<ruby>这儿<rt>Zhèr</rt></ruby><ruby>还<rt>hái</rt></ruby><ruby>有<rt>yǒu</rt></ruby><ruby>水果<rt>shuǐguǒ</rt></ruby>。<ruby>安安<rt>Ān'ān</rt></ruby>，<ruby>给<rt>gěi</rt></ruby><ruby>客人<rt>kèrén</rt></ruby><ruby>削<rt>xiāo</rt></ruby><ruby>苹果<rt>píngguǒ</rt></ruby>。

M: <ruby>您<rt>Nín</rt></ruby><ruby>别<rt>bié</rt></ruby><ruby>忙<rt>máng</rt></ruby><ruby>了<rt>le</rt></ruby>，<ruby>我们<rt>wǒmen</rt></ruby><ruby>自己<rt>zìjǐ</rt></ruby><ruby>来<rt>lái</rt></ruby>。

WM: <ruby>你们<rt>Nǐmen</rt></ruby><ruby>聊<rt>liáo</rt></ruby>，<ruby>我<rt>wǒ</rt></ruby><ruby>去<rt>qù</rt></ruby><ruby>厨房<rt>chúfáng</rt></ruby><ruby>看看<rt>kànkan</rt></ruby>。

J: <ruby>给<rt>Gěi</rt></ruby><ruby>您<rt>nín</rt></ruby><ruby>添<rt>tiān</rt></ruby><ruby>麻烦<rt>máfan</rt></ruby><ruby>了<rt>le</rt></ruby>。

WM: <ruby>哪里<rt>Nǎlǐ</rt></ruby><ruby>哪里<rt>nǎlǐ</rt></ruby>，<ruby>家常便饭<rt>jiācháng-biànfàn</rt></ruby>。<ruby>一会儿<rt>Yíhuìr</rt></ruby><ruby>尝尝<rt>chángchang</rt></ruby><ruby>我<rt>wǒ</rt></ruby><ruby>的<rt>de</rt></ruby><ruby>手艺<rt>shǒuyì</rt></ruby>。

(2) <ruby>在餐桌上<rt>zài cānzhuō shang</rt></ruby>

（<ruby>大家<rt>Dàjiā</rt></ruby><ruby>坐<rt>zuò</rt></ruby><ruby>在<rt>zài</rt></ruby><ruby>饭桌<rt>fànzhuō</rt></ruby><ruby>前<rt>qián</rt></ruby>。）

M: <ruby>做<rt>Zuò</rt></ruby><ruby>了<rt>le</rt></ruby><ruby>这么<rt>zhème</rt></ruby><ruby>多<rt>duō</rt></ruby><ruby>菜<rt>cài</rt></ruby><ruby>啊<rt>a</rt></ruby>！<ruby>您<rt>Nín</rt></ruby><ruby>辛苦<rt>xīnkǔ</rt></ruby><ruby>了<rt>le</rt></ruby>！

WM: <ruby>不<rt>Bù</rt></ruby><ruby>辛苦<rt>xīnkǔ</rt></ruby>，<ruby>就<rt>jiù</rt></ruby><ruby>怕<rt>pà</rt></ruby><ruby>不<rt>bù</rt></ruby><ruby>合<rt>hé</rt></ruby><ruby>你们<rt>nǐmen</rt></ruby><ruby>的<rt>de</rt></ruby><ruby>口味<rt>kǒuwèi</rt></ruby>。

J: <ruby>等等<rt>Děngdeng</rt></ruby>，<ruby>这么<rt>zhème</rt></ruby><ruby>漂亮<rt>piàoliang</rt></ruby><ruby>的<rt>de</rt></ruby><ruby>菜<rt>cài</rt></ruby>，<ruby>我<rt>wǒ</rt></ruby><ruby>先<rt>xiān</rt></ruby><ruby>拍<rt>pāi</rt></ruby><ruby>几<rt>jǐ</rt></ruby><ruby>张<rt>zhāng</rt></ruby><ruby>照片儿<rt>zhàopiānr</rt></ruby>。

WM: Not so spacious, especially when there are many people. Have some tea, please. Help yourselves to some fruit. An'an, peel an apple for your guests.

M: You needn't go to any trouble! We can help ourselves.

WM: Have a good chat. I'll go and take care of things in the kitchen.

J: Sorry to cause so much trouble.

WM: Not at all. It's just home cooking. You'll have a taste a little later.

(2) At the Dining Table

(Everybody is sitting at the table.)

M: So many dishes. You've gone to a lot of trouble.

WM: No, I'm just afraid that you don't like the dishes.

J: Just a moment. They're so beautiful. Let me take a few pictures first.

WF: 来，随便吃点儿吧。
Lái, suíbiàn chī diǎnr ba.

M: 那我们就不客气了。
Nà wǒmen jiù bú kèqi le.

W: 来，尝尝这个板栗鸡块，是我妈妈最拿手的菜。那道过油肉是我爸爸的绝活儿。
Lái, chángchang zhège bǎnlì jīkuài, shì wǒ māma zuì náshǒu de cài. Nà dào guòyóuròu shì wǒ bàba de juéhuór.

M: 你没有露一手？
Nǐ méiyǒu lòu yìshǒu?

W: 有父母在，他们哪会放心让我做！改天给你们吃我做的红烧鸡翅。
Yǒu fùmǔ zài, tāmen nǎ huì fàngxīn ràng wǒ zuò! Gǎitiān gěi nǐmen chī wǒ zuò de hóngshāo jīchì.

(3) 告别
gàobié

M: 时间不早了，我们该回去了。
Shíjiān bù zǎo le, wǒmen gāi huíqù le.

W: 急什么，再坐一会儿吧。
Jí shénme, zài zuò yíhuìr ba.

M: 忙了一天，你们都早点儿休息吧。
Mángle yì tiān, nǐmen dōu zǎo diǎnr xiūxi ba.

WF: Come on, help yourselves.

M: OK, let's not stand on ceremony! Let's eat!

W: Come on, have a piece of this stewed chicken with chestnuts. My mother makes this dish very well. These stir-fried pork slices are my father's specialty.

M: Didn't you cook anything?

W: My parents don't usually let me cook if they're at home. However, I'll prepare braised chicken wings for you another day.

(3) Saying Goodbye

M: It's time for us to be off.

W: Why not stay a little longer?

M: You've been busy the whole day. You all need to have a rest.

W: 对了，你们明天一大早要出发，我就不留你们了。

WF: 慢走啊！

WM: 有时间再来玩儿啊！

M: 一定一定。别送了，请留步！

W: 那我们就不远送了。再见！

W: Oh, and you're leaving early tomorrow morning. I won't keep you now.

WF: Take care.

WM: Come again when you have free time.

M: Of course, of course. No need to see us off. Please stay here!

W: OK. Bye!

New Words

心意	xīnyì	affection; good will; regard
辛苦	xīnkǔ	extremely tired
拿手	náshǒu	be good at
绝活儿	juéhuór	unique skill
露一手	lòu yìshǒu	show off one's skill
出发	chūfā	set off
留步	liúbù	polite word to keep host from seeing you off when leaving

Additional Expressions

Comments on Food

味道好极了！	Wèidao hǎo jí le!	
		The taste is excellent!
有点儿咸。	Yǒudiǎnr xián.	
		It's a bit salty.
太淡了！	Tài dàn le!	
		It's not salty enough.
辣死了！	Làsǐ le!	
		It's too spicy.

Being a Good Guest in China

In China when calling on someone, one must be punctual. Usually one tries to avoid visiting someone at meal times unless invited. In order not to disturb the host, Chinese people do not visit other people in the early morning or within one or two hours after lunch, as some people take a break or even a nap during this time. If visiting some one in the evening one must not stay too long.

It is customary for Chinese people to bring some presents when they call on other people. Cigarettes, wine, fruit and tea are common gifts for the occasion. If there are young children in the family you are visiting, taking some candy or toys that will make both the host and children very happy.

Chinese people usually entertain their guests by preparing tea for them and offering them cigarettes, candy and fruit. If the guests are not invited for a meal in advance, they will take leave before mealtime.

When taking leave, the guest often says, "It's too late and I have to be off." It is customary for the host to try to keep the guest a little longer. When the guest is really leaving, the host usually walks him to the gate and invites the guest to come again another time.

NOTE

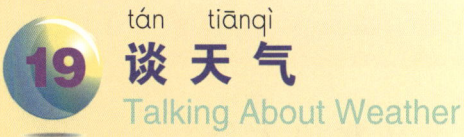

19 tán tiānqì
谈天气
Talking About Weather

Basic Sentences

Jīntiān tiānqì zhēn hǎo!
109. 今天天气真好！
What a nice day it is today!

Míngtiān xiàwǔ kěnéng yǒu léizhènyǔ.
110. 明天下午可能有雷阵雨。
There may be a thunderstorm tomorrow afternoon.

Shíjìshang wǒ zuì xǐhuan dōngtiān le.
111. 实际上我最喜欢冬天了。
In fact, I like winter the best.

Jīntiān tài rè le, zuì gāo qìwēn sānshíbā dù.
112. 今天太热了，最高气温 38 度。
It's too hot today. The high is 38 degrees.

Zhēn ràng rén shòubuliǎo.
113. 真让人受不了。
I can hardly bear it.

Chǎngdì yòu shī yòu huá.
114. 场地又湿又滑。
The court was wet and slippery.

M: 马 克（*Mark*）　W: 王 明（*Wang Ming*）
B: 白 梅（*Bai Mei*）

Dialogues

tánlùn xǐhuan de tiānqì
(1) 谈论喜欢的天气

Jīntiān tiānqì zhēn hǎo!
M: 今天天气真好!

Shì a, tiānqì yì hǎo, xīnqíng jiù hǎo.
W: 是啊,天气一好,心情就好。

Bù zhīdào míngtiān zěnmeyàng. Wǒmen xiǎng qù dǎ gāo'ěrfūqiú.
M: 不知道明天怎么样。我们想去打高尔夫球。

Míngtiān xiàwǔ kěnéng yǒu léizhènyǔ, bié wàngle dài yǔsǎn.
W: 明天下午可能有雷阵雨,别忘了带雨伞。

Yǒudiǎnr yǔ huì bǐjiào liángkuai. Shíjìshang wǒ zuì xǐhuan dōngtiān le.
M: 有点儿雨会比较凉快。实际上我最喜欢冬天了。

Běijīng de dōngtiān yòu lěng yòu gānzào. Búguò Zhōngguó nán běi yǒu hěn dà chāyì. Nánbian de Guǎngzhōu hé běibian de Hā'ěrbīn, dōngtiān wēnchā néng dádào sìshí dù yǐshàng.
W: 北京的冬天又冷又干燥。不过中国南北有很大差异。南边的广州和北边的哈尔滨,冬天温差能达到40度以上。

Shì de, wǒ qùguo Hā'ěrbīn. Zài nàlǐ huáxuě tèbié bàng!
M: 是的,我去过哈尔滨。在那里滑雪特别棒!

(1) Talking About Fine Weather

M: What a nice day it is today!

W: Isn't it? When the weather is nice, people feel happy.

M: I wonder what the weather will be like tomorrow. We want to play golf.

W: There may be a thunderstorm tomorrow afternoon. Don't forget to take an umbrella with you.

M: It'll be cool and pleasant if there is a little rain. In fact, I like winter the best.

W: It's pretty cold and dry in winter in Beijing. The weather in the northern and southern parts of China differs greatly. The difference in temperature of winter between Guangzhou in the south and Harbin in the north is over 40 degrees.

M: You are right. I've been to Harbin. It's terrific to go skiing over there.

(2) 谈论讨厌的天气 tánlùn tǎoyàn de tiānqì

B: 王明，你去看下午的球赛吗？
Wáng Míng, nǐ qù kàn xiàwǔ de qiúsài ma?

W: 去啊！可是今天太热了，最高气温38度。
Qù a! Kěshì jīntiān tài rè le, zuì gāo qìwēn sānshíbā dù.

B: 是啊，这种天气对比赛很不利。最近每天都是这种天气。
Shì a, zhè zhǒng tiānqì duì bǐsài hěn bú lì. Zuìjìn měi tiān dōu shì zhè zhǒng tiānqì.

W: 可能还要持续一个星期。
Kěnéng hái yào chíxù yí gè xīngqī.

B: 真让人受不了。上星期的网球比赛你看了吗？
Zhēn ràng rén shòubuliǎo. Shàng xīngqī de wǎngqiú bǐsài nǐ kàn le ma?

W: 看了。下着雨，场地又湿又滑。
Kàn le. Xiàzhe yǔ, chǎngdì yòu shī yòu huá.

B: 希望今天的天气别影响下午的足球比赛。
Xīwàng jīntiān de tiānqì bié yǐngxiǎng xiàwǔ de zúqiú bǐsài.

W: 天气不好真让球迷着急啊！
Tiānqì bù hǎo zhēn ràng qiúmí zháojí a!

(2) Talking About Terrible Weather

B: Wang Ming, are you going to the ball game this afternoon?

W: Yes, but it's too hot today. The high is 38 degrees.

B: Right. This kind of weather is very bad for the game. The weather has been like this nearly everyday lately.

W: It might go on for another week.

B: I can hardly bear it. Did you go to last week's tennis match?

W: I did. It was raining. The court was wet and slippery.

B: I hope today's weather won't affect the football match this afternoon too much.

W: Bad weather really makes fans upset.

New Words

心情	xīnqíng	mood
雷阵雨	léizhènyǔ	thunderstorm
雨伞	yǔsǎn	umbrella
干燥	gānzào	dry
差异	chāyì	difference
持续	chíxù	continue
影响	yǐngxiǎng	affect
球迷	qiúmí	ball fan

Additional Expressions

Weather

晴	qíng	clear
阴	yīn	overcast
多云	duōyún	cloudy
大风	dà fēng	strong wind
台风	táifēng	typhoon
闷热	mēnrè	hot and stuffy
潮湿	cháoshī	damp
沙尘暴	shāchénbào	sandstorm

China's Climate

China stretches across a vast area, and the continental monsoon climate covers most of it. The country can be further divided into the following climate types:

1. Sub-arctic Coniferous Forest: The northern part of Heilongjiang Province and a small area in the northeastern part of Inner-Mongolia fall into this category. Mohe of Heilongjiang Province is a city typical of this climate.

2. Temperate Steppe Climate: This kind of climate exists along the Inner Mongolian plateau.

3. Temperate Monsoon: Characterized by hot, rainy summers and cold, dry winters, most parts northeast of the Qinling Mountains and Huai River are of this climate.

4. Temperate Desert: The characteristic of this kind of climate is dry, cold in winter and hot in summer, with great variation in temperatures through the year. Most of Xinjiang, except the areas bordering Tibet, are of this type of climate.

5. Sub-tropical Monsoon: This kind of climate is hot and rainy in the summer, mild with little rain in the winter. Most of the area to the southeast of the Qinling Mountains and Huai River as well as Taiwan Island are of this type of climate.

6. Tropical Monsoon: This climate is characterized by high temperatures all the year round, with only two seasons: the dry season and the rainy season. Hainan and Nansha Islands are of this type of climate.

7. Plateau: Temperatures here are lower than areas of the same latitude. The climate varies greatly with different plateau heights. The Qinghai-Tibet Plateau and the Yunnan-Guizhou Plateau are of this type.

20 sòngxíng
送 行
Seeing Off

Basic Sentences

Shíjiān guò de zhēn kuài!
115. 时间过得真快！
How time flies!

Wǒ xīwàng jiānglái yě yǒu jīhuì qù guówài.
116. 我希望将来也有机会去国外。
I hope I'll have a chance to go abroad in the future.

Nǐ zài zhèlǐ de shēnghuó guò de zěnmeyàng?
117. 你在这里的生活过得怎么样？
How do you enjoy your life here?

Shífēn gǎnxiè nǐmen duì wǒ de guānxīn hé zhàogù.
118. 十分感谢你们对我的关心和照顾。
I am very grateful for your consideration and care for me.

Sòng gěi nǐmen zuò gè jìniàn ba.
119. 送给你们做个纪念吧。
Just as a memento.

Zhù dàjiā qiánchéng-sìjǐn!
120. 祝大家前程似锦！
Toast to everybody's bright future!

WA: 王安安 (*Wang An'an*)
M: 马 克 (*Mark*)   B: 白 梅 (*Bai Mei*)
WM: 王 明 (*Wang Ming*)
A: 大 家 (*All*)

Dialogues

(1) 在网上聊天儿
Zài Wǎng Shang Liáotiānr

WA: 马克,我没想到你这么快就要回去了。

M: 是啊,时间过得真快!

WA: 你现在汉语说得和中国人一样好了。

M: 你的法语进步也很大啊。

WA: 我希望将来也有机会去国外。对了,你回家的东西都准备好了吗?

M: 我想去买点儿礼物。你有什么**建议**吗?

WA: 茶叶怎么样?中国人经常互相送茶叶。

(1) Chatting Online

WA: Mark, I didn't expect you would be going back so soon.

M: Ah, how time flies!

WA: You speak Chinese as good as a Chinese person now.

M: You have also made great progress in your French.

WA: I hope I'll have a chance to go abroad in the future. Have you got everything ready for going home?

M: I'd like to buy some presents. Could you give me some suggestions?

WA: What about tea? Chinese people often send tea to one another as gift.

M:茶叶是不错的礼物,不过大多数法国人比较爱喝咖啡。

WA:那你就买点儿容易带的,像丝巾、香扇什么的。

M:最好能买点儿有中国特色的东西。

WA:剪纸、京剧脸谱、中国刺绣、中国风景画都不错。这样吧,等你有空儿的时候我陪你去买。

M:你真是太好了,那我请你吃饭吧。

M: Tea is a good gift, but most French people prefer coffee.

WA: Then you can take something easy to carry, such as silk scarves and fragrant fans.

M: It's better to buy something with Chinese characteristics.

WA: Paper cut, Beijing Opera facial makeup, Chinese embroidery, and Chinese landscape painting are all good. OK, let me go with you one day when you are free, to help you buy.

M: That's kind of you. I'll invite you to dinner.

(2) 和朋友告别

(马克准备回国,白梅准备去广州工作。他们有一个告别聚会。)

B: 时间过得真快!

M: 是啊,欢迎会好像还是昨天的事,今天我们就得说再见了。

WM: 没错!你在这里的生活过得怎么样?

M: 好极了,我交了很多中国朋友。工作也非常顺利。

B: 我的学生都很友好。我还去了不少地方。你们有空的时候可以看看我的博客。

WM: 你还开了中文博客,真了不起!你要去广州了,一定也会喜欢那里的。

(2) Saying Goodbye to Friends

(Mark is going back home and Bai Mei is going to work in Guangzhou. A farewell party is being held in their honor.)

B: How time flies!

M: Yes, it seems we had the welcoming party only yesterday, and we are going to say goodbye today.

WM: Quite right! How do you enjoy your life here?

M: Really enjoy it. I made a lot of Chinese friends. My work has also been quite smooth.

B: My students are very nice. I went to many places. You can vistit my blog when you are free.

WM: It's marvelous that you even began a blog in Chinese. You are going to Guangzhou. You will like the place.

B: 那里的冬天很暖和。你一定要来玩儿。

M: 这是给你们大家的礼物,是我从法国带来的名片盒。十分感谢你们对我的关心和照顾。

WA: 谢谢你,这个名片盒真不错!

WM: 这两个陶瓷杯子送给你们做个纪念吧。

B: 杯子上还有汉字呢,"前程似锦"。

WM. 是啊。让我们干一杯吧。(举起酒杯)祝大家前程似锦!

A: 干杯!

B: It is warm in winter there. You must come and visit me.

M: These gifts are for you. They are business card cases I brought from France. I am very grateful for your consideration and care for me.

WA: Thank you, it is so nice!

WM: These two porcelain cups are for you two, just as a memento.

B: There are Chinese characters on the cups. It means "have a promising future".

WM: Right. Let's drink a toast. *(raising glasses)* Toast to everybody's promising future!

A: Cheers!

New Words

建议	jiànyì	suggestion
陪	péi	accompany
博客	bókè	blog
名片	míngpiàn	business card
照顾	zhàogù	look after; care
陶瓷	táocí	porcelain
纪念	jìniàn	commemorate; memento

Additional Expressions

Tea

绿茶	lǜchá	green tea
花茶	huāchá	scented tea
红茶	hóngchá	black tea
普洱茶	Pǔ'ěrchá	Pu-erh tea, a variety of dark tea
铁观音	Tiěguānyīn	*Tieguanyin*, a variety of oolong tea
菊花茶	júhuāchá	chrysanthemum tea

TIP

Four Treasures of the Study

Chinese unique writing tools, writing brushs (*bi*), ink sticks (*mo*), paper (*zhi*) and ink slabs (*yan*), are known as the four stationary treasures of Chinese study.

Brushes are made of animal hair, such as goat, wolf, or sheep, and are usually attached to a bamboo stick. Their strength depends on which animal hair we used. They can be soft (usually taken from goat), medium (taken from rabbit, or a mixture of goat and weasel hair) or hard and stiff (weasel tail).

Ink sticks are made of pine-soot. There are many processes involved to produce the final product. Such as glue feeding, agent mixing, braizing, moulding, and so on.

The paper included in the Four Treasures of the Study specially refers to Xuan Paper (paper produced in Xuancheng). It is exclusively intended for exercising and creating Chinese calligraphy and painting. Xuan Paper easily absorbs ink and is easy to store. It can maintain flexibility even after a long period of time.

The ink slab is a tool used for grinding the ink stick. A good ink stone is of fine texture and offers other advantages such as quick ink grinding, giving little damage to the hair, is dry-proof, and convenient for cleaning.

In modern times, in order to save time, people write with ready-made ink instead of grinding ink by themselves with the ink stick and ink slab. There is now even a kind of writing thing with which one can write with the effect of a writing brush without dipping in ink.

fùlù
附录

Appendices

I Zhōngguó zhùmíng liánsuǒ jiǔdiàn
中国著名连锁酒店
Well-known Hotel Chains in China

Qītiān Liánsuǒ Jiǔdiàn
七天连锁酒店
Seven Days Inn
✉ http://en.7daysinn.cn

Jiāyuán Liánsuǒ Jiǔdiàn
佳园连锁酒店
Garden Inn
✉ http://www.gardeninns.com.cn

Hàntíng Jiǔdiàn
汉庭酒店
Hanting Inns & Hotels
✉ http://ir.htinns.com

Jǐnjiāngzhīxīng Jiǔdiàn
锦江之星酒店
Jinjiang Inn
✉ http://www.jinjianginns.com

Rújiā Jiǔdiàn
如家酒店
Home Inns Hotel
✉ http://www.homeinns.com

Mòtài Yāoliùbā Liánsuǒ Jiǔdiàn
莫泰１６８连锁酒店
Motel 168 Chain Hotel
✉ http://www.motel168.com

Sù Bā Jiǔdiàn
速８酒店
Super 8 Hotel
✉ http://www.super8.com.cn

Ershísì K Guójì Liánsuǒ Jiǔdiàn
２４K国际连锁酒店
24K Hotels
✉ http://www.24khotels.com

Ānyì Yāowǔbā Liánsuǒ Jiǔdiàn
安逸１５８连锁酒店
Ane 158 Hotel
✉ http://www.158hotel.com

fùlù
附录
Appendices

II Běijīng gè lèi shìchǎng
北京各类市场
Various Markets in Beijing

Clothing

Xiùshuǐjiē Fúzhuāng Shìchǎng
秀水街服装市场
Silk Market
✉ Yong'anli, Jianguomenwai Dajie, Chaoyang Qu
☎ 010-51698880

Dòngwùyuán Xīntiāndì Fúzhuāng Pīfā Shìchǎng
动物园新天地服装批发市场
New World Clothing Wholesale Market near Beijing Zoo
✉ 116 Xiwai Dajie, Xicheng Qu
☎ 010-68356797

Guānyuán Shāngpǐn Pīfā Shìchǎng
官园商品批发市场
Guanyuan Commodity Wholesale Market
✉ 4 Chegongzhuang Dajie, Xicheng Qu
☎ 010-51954001

Antiques

Běijīng Gǔwánchéng
北京古玩城
Beijing Curio City
✉ 21 Dongsanhuan Nanlu, Chaoyang Qu
☎ 010-59609999

Liàngmǎ Guójì Zhūbǎo GǔwánChéng
亮马国际珠宝古玩城
Liangma International Jewel and Antique Market
✉ 27 Liangmaqiao Lu. Chaoyang Qu
☎ 010-64679664

Pānjiāyuán Jiùhuò Shìchǎng
潘家园旧货市场
Panjiayuan Antique Market
✉ 18 Huaweili Panjiayuan Lu, Chaoyang Qu
☎ 010-51204673

Household Products

Tiānyì Shìchǎng
天意市场
Tianyi Market
✉ 259 Fuwai Dajie, Xicheng Qu
☎ 010-68329332

Jīnwǔxīng Bǎihuò Pīfāchéng
金五星百货批发城
Jinwuxing General Merchandise Wholesale Market
✉ Beisanhuan Sidaokou, Haidian Qu
☎ 010-62226829

Electronics

Hǎilóng Diànzǐchéng
海龙电子城
Hailong Electronics Market
✉ 1 Zhongguancun Dajie, Haidian Qu
☎ 400-600-0099

Běijīng Guīgǔ Diànnǎochéng
北京硅谷电脑城
Beijing Silicon Valley Computer Plaza
✉ 1 Xicaochang, Haidian Qu
☎ 010-82852662

Bǎinǎohuì Diànnǎo Shìchǎng
百脑汇电脑市场
Buynow Computer Market
✉ 99 Chaowai Dajie, Chaoyang Qu
☎ 010-58761588

Dǐnghǎo Diànzǐ Shāngchéng
鼎好电子商城
Dinghao Electronics City
✉ 3 Haidian Dajie, Haidian Qu
☎ 800-810-7168

Others

Yùquányíng Huāhuì Shìchǎng
玉泉营花卉市场
Yuquanying Flower Market
✉ 55 Nansanhuan Xilu, Fenggtai Qu
☏ 010-64898106

Mǎliándào Cháchéng
马连道茶城
Maliandao Tea Street
✉ 11 Maliandao Lu, Xicheng Qu
☏ 010-51920098

Běijīng Túshū Pīfā Shìchǎng
北京图书批发市场
Beijing Wholesale Book Market
✉ 16 Tianshuiyuan Beili, Chaoyang Qu
☏ 010-65062680

Běijīng Shèyǐng Qìcáichéng
北京摄影器材城
Beijing Photographic Equipment City
✉ 40 Wukesong Lu, Haidian Qu
☏ 010-88119723